D0321636

THE CONVENTION ON THE FUTURE OF EUROPE

Working Towards an EU Constitution

Jo Shaw,
Paul Magnette,
Lars Hoffmann
& Anna Vergés Bausili

THE FEDERAL TRUST
for education & research

ISBN 1 903403 60 X

We are grateful to the London Office of the European Parliament for supporting the publication of this book.

NOTE: All contributors to this volume are writing in a personal capacity. Views expressed are those of the authors and do not represent the position of their institution.

This book is the sixth title in the Federal Trust series *Future of European Parliamentary Democracy*. The previous volumes are available from the publisher: *Seven Theorems in Search of the European Parliament* (1999, 0 901573 70 1) by David Coombes; *What Next for the European Parliament* (1999, 0 901573 90 6) by Andreas Mauer, *Shaping Europe: Reflections of Three MEPs* (2000, 0 901573 99 X) by Lord Plumb, Carole Tongue and Florus Wijsenbeek; *Choice and Representation in the European Union* (2003, 0 901573 73 6) edited by Roger Morgan and Michael Steed; and *Europe, Parliaments and the Media* (forthcoming, 1 903403 22 7) edited by Martyn Bond.

The Federal Trust is a Registered Charity No. 272241
7 Graphite Square, Vauxhall Walk,
London SE11 5EE
Company Limited by Guarantee No.1269848

Marketing and Distribution by Kogan Page Ltd
Printed by J W Arrowsmith Ltd

Contents

About the authors

Lars Hoffmann is a research officer at the Federal Trust working on the project 'Constitutionalism, Federalism and Reform of the EU'. He has worked on legitimacy and institutional issues of the EU reform process and currently works on the Convention-method and CFSP.

Paul Magnette is a professor for political science at the Université Libre de Bruxelles where he is also the director of the Institut d'études européennes. In addition he teaches at the Institute d'Études Politique in Paris. His Research focuses on institutional dimensions of the EU and democratic theory. He has published on European citizenship, the constitutionalisation of the EU and questions of accountability and legitimacy in the EU.

Jo Shaw has been Professor of European Law and Jean Monnet Chair at the University of Manchester since September 2001 and is also a Senior Research Fellow at the Federal Trust since October 2001 directing the EU Constitution Project on 'Constitutionalism, Federalism and the Reform of the European Union'. Jo Shaw has widely published in the field of the EU constitution and institutions, particularly in socio-legal and interdisciplinary perspective.

Anna Vergés Bausili is a research officer at the Federal Trust working on the project 'Constitutionalism, Federalism and Reform of the EU'. She is currently working on the theme of division of powers. In 2001 was Research Fellow at the Centre for European Studies at the University of Limerick researching on convergence and cohesion in the EU.

Foreword
Brendan Donnelly

Ever since its founding in 1945, the Federal Trust has sought to place itself at the heart of the debate in this country on European questions. The following book stands squarely within this proud tradition, being timely, authoritative and thought-provoking. At one level, it is a report on work in progress at the European Union's Constitutional Convention, chaired by Valéry Giscard d'Estaing. At another, it sets the groundwork for a more general historical and conceptual analysis of the whole European constitutionalisation process, of which Giscard's Convention is only the most contemporary part. It is this latter aspect of the book which will ensure its continued relevance and usefulness long after the Convention has finished its work.

It is entirely appropriate that a number of hands from the Federal Trust should have contributed to this volume. The Constitutional Convention is the product of a number of over-lapping agendas, and the differences in focus between the various chapters of this book well reflect this fact. Clarity, simplicity, transparency, efficiency and legitimacy are all undeniably desirable attributes of any constitution. But it is often easier to advocate than to achieve the melding together of all these values in an overarching constitutional construction. This problem is particularly acute in a case like that of the European Union, where a considerable, if uncodified corpus of constitutional practice and theory already exists. The Convention is not starting from a blank sheet of paper. Part at least of its task is to make sense and coherence out of the differing, sometimes conflicting tendencies which legally and politically have shaped the European Union until now.

At the time of writing, we cannot be certain to what extent the present Constitutional Convention will succeed in influencing the detailed provisions of the Treaty that precedes the next wave of the European Union's enlargement. But it would be a mistake to see the Convention's work simply in terms of its immediate impact on national ministers in an Intergovernmental Conference. If nothing else, the Convention has served as a useful stock-taking of just how far the European Union has already proceeded along the road of constitutional integration. This has been a surprise to many, pleasant or disagreeable according to taste. After Giscard's Convention, further steps along the European constitutional road will certainly be taken with greater consciousness of the issues involved. This cannot but make the European debate more transparent and its conclusions correspondingly more legitimate. This book is written in a similar spirit. It seeks to analyse and illuminate at least as much as to persuade and recommend.

Brendan Donnelly
Director of the Federal Trust
May 2003

Introduction
Jo Shaw, Lars Hoffmann
and Anna Vergés Bausili

It might seem foolhardy to stand back and attempt objective comment about a radical process of change such as the Future of Europe debate, and specifically the work of the Convention on the Future of the Union, whilst it is still ongoing. It might be thought that this type of undertaking is ultimately the preserve of short-lived commentary alone, especially that found hitherto primarily in newspapers and magazines, but now increasingly made available with astonishing international immediacy via the internet. Instead of replicating that laudable work, the essays in this book take a rather longer view, placing the debates in wider context, by focusing on key questions about the legitimacy of the EU, about constitutional change and constitution-building, and about how and what the EU does as an emergent polity.

This is not strictly an editorial introduction, as this is a co-authored rather than an edited work. Three of the papers, those by Hoffmann, Shaw and Vergés-Bausili, originate in the Federal Trust's ongoing study on Constitutionalism, Federalism and the Reform of the European Union ('EU Constitution Project').[1] These papers have all evolved on the basis of close collaboration and interchange between the authors. The fourth paper, by Magnette, although nominally an outsider at the dinner table, fits so closely this book's attempt to examine the interactions between innovation and acquis, between the new and the old, and to question how and whether the EU is 'working towards' a constitution, that the 'joins' are barely visible.

Unlike an editorial introduction, which often has the task of linking diverse contributions to a central theme, the introduction will not summarise the papers, whose relationship to the role of the Convention in the constitution-building process could hardly be clearer. Instead, since none of the chapters is directly dedicated to presenting an exposition of the Convention, the introduction takes up this task. The book as a whole is not intended to review the Convention's work, to present the options which it has before it, to chart the emergence of consensus amongst its members, and to predict its final outcomes, although those points are briefly brought out below. It should be recalled, however, that any such conclusions are necessarily provisional when written before the Convention reported, and before the subsequent Intergovernmental Conference ('IGC') started its work. Final assessments of the Convention as political process and as a forum for constitution-building, as well as complete reviews of how it negotiated its way through the complex highways and byways presented by the many options put before it, and why and with what effects it made the choices it did, will come later.

The establishment of a Convention on the Future of Europe represents, in absolute terms, a step forward in the democratisation of the EU, that is in relation to previous exercises of treaty revision. On the other hand, in relative terms, the evaluation of the dynamics and outcomes of the Convention is clearly a matter of discussion.

At its meeting in Laeken in December 2001, the European Council convened a Convention on the Future of the European Union. The task of the Convention was to prepare the way for the next Intergovernmental Conference (to be convened in 2003-2004) as broadly and openly as possible. The background to this historic decision can be found in a number of sources.

The decision to run a new round of reform was first made before the previous IGC (Nice 2000) was concluded. In good measure operating according to the logics of path-dependency, a substantial part of the agenda of the 2004 IGC was already drawn at the 2000 IGC which had proved unable to reach a satisfactory agreement on a number of items, especially matters related to institutional reform. Thus the Declaration no. 23 annexed to the Treaty of Nice pinpointed four questions in particular that ought to be addressed by the Convention (the role of national parliaments, the simplification of the treaties (at that time, without changing their meaning), the status of the charter of fundamental rights, and a more precise delimitation of powers between the EU and member states).

The post-Nice process, with the launching of the debate on the Future of Europe, did however broaden the Nice 'shopping list'. Under the Swedish and Belgian Presidencies, the post-Nice process developed into a more thorough revision exercise than some governments were probably at the time thinking they wished to see. At an informal meeting of the European Council in Ghent (October 2001) the guidelines were agreed for the establishment of a Convention to deal with substantial institutional and constitutional matters left-over from previous rounds of treaty reform, and finally in December 2001 the Laeken Declaration, which originated in the Conclusions of the Nice European Council, broadened the four points earmarked at Nice into a larger institutional and even constitutional agenda.

Besides being part of a new scheduled grand-bargain to examine a number of left-overs and a broader set of issues, the post-Nice process (including the setting up of the Convention on the Future of Europe) represents a qualitatively different round, notably a more participatory and open exercise. While the experience of the Convention of Fundamental Rights and Freedoms must have contributed positively to the choice for the Convention method, other factors such as the first (failed) ratification referendum of the Nice Treaty in Ireland in October 2001 may have fuelled the defenders of a more deliberative forum for grand Treaty reform.

The task of the Convention, as set out in the Laeken Declaration, was to:

'consider the key issues arising for the Union's future development and to try to identify the various possible responses.'

Thus the Convention was asked to consider the key issues arising for the Union's future development, such as:

• What do European citizens expect from the Union?

• How is the division of competences between the Union and the member states to be organised?

• Within the Union, how is the division of powers between the institutions to be organised?

- How can the efficiency and coherence of the Union's external action be ensured?

- How can the Union's democratic legitimacy be ensured?

Although a choice for institutional autonomy on the part of the Convention was not apparently originally envisaged,[2] the Laeken Declaration did ask the Convention to 'draw up a final document, which may comprise either different options, indicating the degree of support which they received, or recommendations, if consensus is achieved.' Recommendations agreed by consensus would clearly hold strong political weight, and this is what the Convention – under the guidance of its Chair, ex-French President Valéry Giscard d'Estaing – explicitly worked towards from the very beginning, in drawing up a single draft of a Constitutional Treaty. It can be anticipated that Giscard will work until he has found a text which by and large can be accepted by the majority of the 'mainstream' Convention members, although it can be anticipated that the euro-sceptic or euro-critical minority may decide to issue a minority report. More serious for Giscard would be the failure to bridge the differences between, for example, a pro-EU 'British' view and mainstream 'continental federalism', which is particularly prominent amongst the institutional 'insiders' in the Convention, namely the Commission and European Parliamentary members of the Convention.

However, whatever the Convention agrees, this is not the end of the matter. There must be an IGC to conclude any treaty reform, followed eventually by national ratification in accordance with the respective constitutional requirements of the individual member states. In other words, any change and indeed abrogation of the existing Treaties must be agreed unanimously in accordance with the provisions of Article 48 TEU. Whether all member states would then agree to join the new project, which will probably still be called the 'European Union', and whether any *further* changes would require unanimous or only majority approval, is a matter which the Convention and later the IGC must decide.

The Heads of State and Government agreed at Laeken that a period of a few months should separate the end of the Convention and the beginning of the IGC. It should be recalled, in any event, that the Convention was envisaged originally to last *just one year*, so that it should have been finished by March 2003, having begun its deliberations on 28 February 2002. In fact, the Convention soon gave signs of developing some life of its own: the Convention's timetable was quickly extended to reach the end of the Greek Presidency in June 2003, and the crisis over Iraq has been one of the factors indicating that it may have to labour longer and harder to achieve consensus over some sticking points such as institutional design, the Common Foreign and Security Policy, and the extent and nature of any Defence Policy. In addition, the Convention's desire to provide a complete and bespoke solution for the IGC to take up, which has led it also to undertake a process of review of what is now called 'Part Two' of the Constitutional Treaty, namely the detailed sections on policies, legal bases and institutional arrangements, has made its work more complex and more extensive. From February 2003 onwards, there were indications that many in the Convention would like to meet again after the summer 2003 recess. These hopes were conclusively dashed by the European Council in April 2003, which called for the trial report for its Thessaloniki meeting on 20/21 June 2003.

Turning to the linkage between the IGC and the Convention, various scenarios can be envisaged. The Convention is likely to structure to some extent the agenda of the IGC[3] but those wanting to harness the momentum of the Convention, and wishing to avoid a situation in which the member states feel free to disturb what was decided in the Convention, obviously favour a quick turnaround between Convention and IGC, as well as retention of the timetable based on a June completion.[4] Furthermore, the Italian Government has long hankered after the possibility that the new foundational treaty could be a second Treaty of Rome, concluded under the Italian Presidency of the second half of 2003. On the other hand, enlargement will only be formally concluded – for those states which approve their accession treaties – in May 2004, which suggests that for any new treaty to be concluded by all the relevant and affected states, it would be essential to delay any formal signing until after that time, even if the ink was by then dried on the text. Furthermore, a number of accession states, supported in the Convention by national parliamentary voices such as the UK parliament representatives, as well as Ireland and Sweden,[5] have argued for the retention of the original timetable incorporating a 'reflection phase' between Convention and IGC, in part to give the accession states more time to separate out the two major issues of accession and constitutional change.[6] It is very clear that the issue of the timetable is closely linked to the question of legitimacy, and in particular the potential role of a transnational referendum potentially coinciding with the European Parliament elections in June 2004 as the basis for seeing whether the new Constitutional Treaty can receive widespread public approval.[7] Momentum towards a successful transnational ratification referendum (whether advisory or binding in individual states) could offer substantial legitimacy benefits for the European Union.

As noted already, the Convention is headed by Giscard d'Estaing as Chair or President. The rest of a three-person Presidency appointed in the Laeken Declaration comprises Jean-Luc Dehaene and Guiliano Amato as Vice-Presidents. Both are former Prime Ministers (of Belgium and Italy respectively). In addition, the Laeken Declaration envisaged the following composition:

- Fifteen representatives of the national governments of the member states
- Thirty representatives of the national parliaments of the member states
- Sixteen representatives of the European Parliament
- Two representatives of the European Commission.

The three-person Presidency is not included amongst these representatives. They do not 'represent' anyone. They are intended to be an independent motor and framework for the Convention.

The Laeken Declaration also envisaged candidate country representation on the same basis for the twelve countries then negotiating accession, plus Turkey which has candidate country status, but which has not yet begun negotiations:

- Thirteen representatives of the national governments of the candidate countries
- Twenty-six representatives of the national parliaments of the candidate countries

However, according to the Laeken Declaration the candidate country representatives are not in a position to prevent a consensus emerging, and although one of their number is a 'member' of the Praesidium, which effectively 'runs' the Convention, he is there as a 'guest' rather than as a full member. On the other hand, in many respects candidate country representatives have participated as fully as any others in the deliberations of the Convention, and there were strong arguments that after the formal signing of the accession treaties on 16 April 2003, from which date the accession countries would have active observer status in all EU institutions, that the status of the representatives of the ten countries in question should be formally equated to those of the existing member states.

In addition to members, there are observers:

- Three observers from the Economic and Social Committee
- Six observers from the Committee of the Regions
- Three observers representing the social partners
- The European Ombudsman.

Each member of the Convention is shadowed by an alternate or substitute, effectively doubling the numbers involved. These members likewise have more or less full participation rights, especially in the context of Working Group discussions. There is not equal representation of nationalities in the Convention, as positions such as Commission or European Parliament representative were not distributed by nationality, and the Presidency members do not count towards national delegations. France is best represented, although for their size Portugal and Belgium both have large delegations, in each case outnumbering the Spanish delegation.[8]

The membership of the Convention has remained by no means static. For example, it is a testimony to the Convention's success in finding a consensus basis for a draft Constitutional Treaty that many Governments have gradually replaced their national representatives with more senior political figures.[9] By April 2003, there were five Foreign Ministers and two Deputy Prime Ministers amongst the Convention members. While this made the Convention more like an IGC in certain respects, indicating that the member states were clearly taking its deliberations seriously, it ultimately gave no clue as to whether the member states would find themselves almost completely 'locked into' any consensus solution recommended by the Convention, or rather were preparing the ground to circumvent the Convention's findings.

The Praesidium of the Convention is composed of the three members of the Presidency, two representatives from the European Parliament, the Commission, and the national parliaments, the representatives of the three governments holding the Presidency of the

EU during the lifetime of the Convention (Spain, Denmark, Greece), and – as noted above – one 'guest' representing the accession countries. In some cases (Ireland for instance) governments have to rely on nationality networks to influence the work of the Praesidium (Bruton is different party than Ahern). According to the Laeken Declaration the function of the Praesidium was to 'lend impetus' to the Convention, and to provide it 'with an initial working basis'. From the beginning, the Praesidium was effectively the decision-making body of the Convention, e.g. adopting the Convention's Rules of Procedure – although the extent to which these were truly collective decisions, or rather came more from the President of the Convention imposing his will – is a moot point. Members of the Praesidium chaired all the Working Groups and the Discussion Circles, allowing them to control the agendas of these forums for discussion to a substantial degree. As the work of the Convention progressed, the Praesidium also transmuted into a drafting body, debating and approving the release of tranches of articles for discussion in plenary, and for the individual Convention members to comment upon and produce amendments. The Praesidium has been a rather secretive body, since it does not produce minutes of its meetings. It has been suggested that it is overall rather ineffective as it is relatively unpoliticised, and could easily be dominated by the Presidency and by the Secretariat, headed by ex-UK diplomat Sir John Kerr. On the other hand, there is evidence primarily of an anecdotal nature that Praesidium members have consistently contested aspects of the lead given by Giscard and indeed by Kerr, in relation to questions such as working methods, the contents of articles, and the nature of meetings, which increased in both frequency and length.

Giscard took the lead in one area by suggesting that the Convention work in three phrases: a listening phase (through to summer 2002), a phase of analysis, focused around Working Group discussions and reports (summer, autumn and winter 2002), and a third phase of drawing together the different proposals and drafting recommendations, which began in early 2003. In addition, Giscard substantially shaped the nature of the Convention's debates by decreeing that institutional questions should be discussed towards the end, and were not included in the listening phase or the analysis phase at all. This dismayed Convention members who felt that it was impossible to have substantive and sensible discussions about issues such as External Action or Defence, unless one knew what the institutional options in terms of leadership and the capacity for executive action might actually be. On the other hand, from the beginning Giscard knew that institutional questions would deeply divide the Convention members, and he sought to keep a lid on this particular conflict for as long as possible.

Certain aspects of the Convention's dynamics were shaped in a decisive way from the beginning. These included the public nature of plenary sessions, the full availability of documentation via the website, and the structured – if not always successful – consultation with civil society, via the Forum and its website and via a specially convened plenary session in June 2002. On the other hand, in many respects for civil society lobbying the Convention has been much like business as usual, involving contacts with sympathetic members and targeted distribution of materials presenting their arguments. National civil society debates have, in most member states, been conspicuous by their absence. In addition to the involvement of civil society, there was a shadow Youth Convention in July 2002. In terms of the dynamics as they have evolved, some preliminary observations can be ventured. The Convention has been, on the whole, more presidential than parliamentary, with substantial central control. Even so, party political dynamics have been quite strong, with active caucusing in the European party federations. The different sizeable delegations – national government representatives, national parliament representatives, European Parliament representatives – have taken differing amounts of time to gel as effective groups. Clearly, the European Parliament members of the Convention had a substantial headstart, since meetings were taking place in their own place of work. National parliament representatives have perhaps found the terrain most difficult, especially since the travelling is probably most burdensome for them, and many may be poorly supported by logistical, technical and expert help. On the other hand, the evidence of many contributions from Convention members indicate cross-delegation discussions are active, and many integrate the national parliamentary representatives very successfully, for example in relation to issues such as the Convention/IGC timetable.

In October 2002, the Praesidium issued a skeleton draft Constitutional Treaty,[10] which many observers felt was strongly marked by the specific influence of Giscard's ideas, for example, in its refusal to rule out the institution of a Congress of the People, which was an idea which had not attracted much support in plenary debates.[11] This has structured subsequent debate, and the successive tranches of articles which have been issued since February 2003 have essentially followed the framework established in that document, effectively fleshing it out.[12] This means that the ordinary Convention members had little chance to change some of the foundational architectural features of the draft Constitutional Treaty, such as the order of different sections, and the decision to have one article on values, one on objectives, and so on. Furthermore, the numerous drafts of model constitutions or treaties which have been presented by or sponsored by Convention members appear to have had little influence over the shape chosen by the Praesidium.[13] In March 2003, the Convention began to have additional and more informal plenary meetings, which were intended to increase the pace of debate and provide opportunities for more effective interchange amongst members, rather than the posturing of set piece speeches which too often undermined the effectiveness of the debate in the 'ordinary' plenary sessions. In the absence of a full set of preliminary articles, and bearing in mind the plethora of amendments which were rapidly presented by Convention members – most famously more than 1000 for the first sixteen draft articles – the best way to judge the emerging consensus was to take particular account of the eleven Working Group reports and more than twenty plenary debates on particular issues.[14]

Consensus was apparent on structural legal questions, such as elimination of the framework, if not the effects, of the Maastricht pillar system, and on the incorporation of the Charter of Fundamental Rights as a constitutional document. That leaves aside, however, many detailed questions which are not resolved.[15] Areas of greater (e.g. justice and home affairs) and lesser agreement (e.g. categorisation of competences, socio-economic governance and common foreign and security policy (CFSP)) had become apparent in relation to the question of what the Union should do, and how it should do it. On institutions, while influential proposals were on the table from groups of large and small member states, many of which contrasted sharply with the conclusions implicit or explicit in Working Group reports such as those on External Action and Defence, Convention members were forced to play a waiting game being unable to anticipate what the Praesidium would come up with by way of draft articles.[16] Even in relation to one institutional question which *was* explicitly and extensively discussed in Working Groups, namely the role of national parliaments, deep divisions rather than consensus remained evident about this question. It is one thing piously to declare that to involve national parliaments better in scrutinising European legislation, and especially in relation to the question of monitoring the application of the subsidiarity principle, would help bridge the EU's legitimacy gap and bring it 'closer' to the peoples of the member states, but quite another to find effective and workable mechanisms for doing this.[17]

At the end of the day, the Convention may end up being not much more than a dignified preparatory stage. The capacity of the Convention to lead seems slim at a time when there is need for leadership and political will (Iraq and the response by some member states to have a mini summit on defence seem to show that). The composition of the Convention may in fact be detrimental to its capacity to achieve political results – even though it will undoubtedly bring improvements in some areas (such as structuring the agenda for the Convention with some consensus in less controversial areas, and enhancing the democratic credentials of the review process).

This introduction has set the scene for the four substantive chapters on the evolving European constitution which follow. It has provided a brief and preliminary assessment of the Convention, how it works and some of what it has done. Simplification was supposed to be a *leitmotiv* of the Convention. In fact, the challenge of following and assessing its work has become a complex task. Furthermore, what it may propose for the European Union may, in truth, be little simplified on what has preceded it. Those *caveats* notwithstanding, the Convention has offered a unique engagement on the part of the set of European elites with the constitutional question for the European Union. The chapters which follow will elaborate in much more detail upon that theme.

Notes

[1] Much of the presentation which follows draws upon the work of the Federal Trust EU Constitution Project. For more details see website (http://www.fedtrust.co.uk/eu_constitution).

[2] See point 6 of the Draft Minutes of the General Affairs Council held on 8 October 2001 (Document 12551/01) where is indicated clearly that the Convention brief was originally one of presenting options for the 2004 IGC (like the 1996 Reflection Group)

rather than preparing a single document with no brackets.

[3] A number of defining agreements had already been achieved in the Convention by Spring 2003 (Crum 2003) while clearly distributional and power related issues are less likely to be solved by the Convention.

[4] 'The Convention and the timetable of the Intergovernmental Conference', CONV 626/ 03, CONTRIB 280, 19 March 2003. Contribution promoted by Convention members Duff and Dini, but supported by a number of members from the accession states.

[5] 'IGC date causes convention split', EU Observer 28.02.2003; www.euobserver.com.

[6] 'On the full participation of the acceding states in the European Convention, and on the timing of the Intergovernmental Conference to follow', CONV 566/83, CONTRIB 252, 19 February 2003, pleading for a reflection period, but allowing for flexibility in the timings. See also 'Keep the IGC Timetable from Nice and Laeken', CONV 599/03, CONTRIB 268, 6 March 2003.

[7] See the well supported contribution: 'Referendum on the European Constitution', CONV 658/03, CONTRIB 291, 31 March 2003.

[8] See Closa, 2003: 6, based on data prepared by Ben Crum, CEPS.

[9] Strictly speaking, national government representatives are the personal representatives of the Heads of State and Government of the member states – i.e. the members of the European Council. This allowed a great variety of representation amongst the original nominees, ranging from Foreign Ministers (e.g. Belgium), to non-politically active academics (e.g. Finland), via senior officials and European Parliament members (e.g. Spain – although Ana Palacio, the person in question, was subsequently made Spanish Foreign Minister, left the European Parliament and swapped from being 'full' to 'alternate' member, doubtless in view of the Convention workload).

[10] CONV 369/02 of 28 October 2002.

[11] For an analysis see Shaw, 2002.

[12] CONV 528/03 of 6 February 2003 (Articles 1-16); CONV 571/03 of 26 February 2003 (Articles 24-33); CONV 602/03 of 14 March 2003 (Articles on finance); CONV 614/03 of 14 March 2003 (Articles on freedom, security and justice); CONV 647/03 of 2 April 2003 (Part Three: General and Final Provisions); CONV 648/03 of 2 April 2003 (Articles 43-46; Union membership); CONV 649/03 of 2 April 2003 (Article 42: Union and its immediate environment); CONV 650/03 of 2 April 2003 (Articles 33-37; democratic life of the Union).

[13] For links to the texts, see http://www.fedtrust.co.uk/constit_draftconstitutions.htm

[14] See for example Crum, 2003 and the periodic assessments by Stanley Crossick on the European Policy Centre website: www.theepc.be

[15] See Shaw in this volume.

[16] See the fears expressed in relation to the institutional debate resulting from the lack of clarity in the Praesidium's approach in Hughes, 2003.

[17] See Weatherill, 2003a.

Will the EU be more legitimate after the Convention?

Paul Magnette[1]

Since the ratification of the Maastricht Treaty at the beginning of the 1990s, the problem of the EU's 'democratic legitimacy' has been one of the most discussed aspects of European integration, both in academia and in the real world. The Laeken Declaration, giving birth to the Convention on the Future of the Union, bears witness to this widespread public preoccupation when it presents the question of democratic legitimacy as 'the first challenge facing Europe'. The creation of the Convention itself, conceived as a broad and open body, is supposed to be an element of answer to this challenge; the questions its members are asked to discuss cover a broad range of subjects, but all of them are said to be related to the EU's democratic ambition; the plenary sessions of the Convention confirm that its members pay tribute – or at least pretend to pay tribute – to this objective: most of their interventions are based on the argument that the reform they support is connected to democratic intentions.

In spite (or because) of the consensus on the importance of the question, the mission of the Convention is a very difficult one. Giving an answer to the question of what a 'democratic Union' could be indeed supposes an agreement on the meaning of democracy and on the nature of the EU. Ten years of discussions on these two controversial questions have shown that conflicts of interpretations among European leaders and public opinion remain very deep. In order to reach its purpose, the Convention will have to reduce this dissonance, and to forge a common understanding, not only among leaders but also among the general public, of these basic constitutional principles.

In the first section of this chapter, I briefly recall the *conflict of interpretations* over the EU's democratic legitimacy and argue that the EU is not a simple 'modus vivendi' and its basic rules are more controversial than those of a 'constitutional consensus' defined in Rawls' terms. I will then, in the second part, focus on the *process* of the Convention and argue that its deliberative nature might be a (modest) contribution to the democratic legitimation of the European Union. In the last section, I examine the *likely outcome* of the Convention, in terms of policies and institutions, and underline the aspect of the present conflicts of interpretation that it will probably not be able to solve. I nevertheless conclude that the EU can live with these ambiguities, and that its legitimacy will be strengthened if the Convention manages to forge a consensus on some formal core issues.

The conflict of standards

One of the reasons why the debate on the EU's democratic legitimacy remains so lively is that the diagnosis of the different actors and scholars, and the suggestions they made, are based on different assumptions, which are rarely made clear.[2] In this continuous controversy, scholars classically distinguish five different vectors of legitimation.[3]

Indirect legitimacy

According to this notion, the legitimacy of the European Union can at best be indirect or derivative. It depends on the legitimacy of its component states, its respect for their sovereignty, and its ability to serve their purposes. Supported by the German Constitutional Court in its famous decision on the Maastricht Treaty, this argument is the *leitmotiv* of those who, within and outside the Convention, defend an intergovernmental vision of the Union. In the academic literature, this rationalist assumption is also associated with principal-agent models, according to which any autonomy of Union institutions is not evidence of their independent legitimacy, but of where it suits states to confer limited discretion on a supranational agent, according to a contract that is contingent, calculated and controlled.

According to this argument, the EU would be a democratic polity if its competences were defined in strict terms and if national parliaments were given the opportunity to control the action of their governments acting in the Council and the growth of EU competences.

Federal legitimacy

A second classic view is that the Union can only be democratic if it follows the traditional devices of federalism. Constantly defended by the Commission, by the majority of the EP since its direct election in 1979, as well as by Germany and the Benelux countries, and recently advocated by Jürgen Habermas,[4] this argument is based on an orthodox Madisonian reasoning. A polity that is territorially segmented, yet focussed on the management of problems that cut across those sub-units, will require representative structures that can aggregate and deliberate on preferences both nationally and transnationally. The need for dual legitimation might also be justified by the classic argument for mixed government. If it is unlikely that rational citizens will consent for long to systems of rule that expose them to risks of arbitrary domination, a legitimate Union cannot afford to concentrate power, whether in a club of governments or in a parliamentary majority, but must, instead, institutionalise checks and balances between the carriers of those two legitimacy claims.

Practically, the advocates of this federal vision support the authority of the Commission and the powers of the European Parliament, as counterweights to the international nature of the Council. They tend to see the Commission as a federal government, that should be personalised to help citizens perceive the issues of EU politics.

Technocratic Legitimacy

According to this perspective, the EU is legitimated as an 'independent fourth branch of government'.[5] This position implies the following: first, a normative belief that the superior ability of a system to meet citizen needs is grounds for political obligation to it; second, epistemological confidence in a rationality or science of government (positivism); and, third the identification of specific public needs that can only be met by independent European institutions.

Though this argument is rarely voiced as such in the political arena, and never presented as a comprehensive doctrine of legitimacy, it underlies the status of the European Central Bank and of other agencies, including the Commission in some of its tasks.

Procedural Legitimacy

Though it can be seen as a vector in itself, procedural legitimacy is often presented in the EU literature as a means of filling a gap in technocratic legitimacy. In response to criticisms that independent technocratic agencies are means of escaping democratic controls, some authors have defended a procedural conception, according to which the legitimacy of an action rests in its observance of certain formal procedures: transparency, motivation, balance of interests, evaluation, participation of stakeholders and so on.[6] Moreover, from this formal point of view, what gives the Union legal legitimacy is not just its attentiveness to due process, but also its capacity to generate an original normative order that confers new rights and entitlements on citizens, enforceable even against states themselves.

Corporate legitimacy

Another way of securing the legitimacy of a policy is by negotiating it directly with those whose compliance it needs. Such an approach may confer legitimacy where it is generally accepted that those exposed to the concentrated effects of public policy should have special rights of consultation in the decision-making process. Although the corporatist ideas that lay, for example, behind the creation of the Economic and Social Committee (ECOSOC) have little purchase on contemporary economy and society, the Commission has sought new ways of identifying those affected by its policies and including them in their design.[7]

By way of summary, it is useful to show how each vector of legitimacy implies its own distinct account of what is needed to make the EU legitimate on the input and output sides of governance.[8] In the case of indirect legitimacy, authorisation by member states and the delivery of state preferences are the sources of input and output legitimacy respectively. In that of federal legitimacy, elections provide input legitimacy and the delivery of voter preferences secures output legitimacy. In the case of technocratic legitimacy expertise and delivery of efficiency are the key inputs and outputs. In that of procedural legitimacy, due process is a source of input legitimacy, whilst output legitimacy is constituted by the delivery of rights. Under corporate legitimacy consultation and compliance of organised actors are indicators of input and output legitimacy respectively.

Input and output legitimacy under the five vectors

Vectors of legitimation	Input	Output
Indirect	Authorisation	State preference
Federal	Elections	Voters' preference
Technocratic	Expertise	Efficiency
Procedural	Due process	Rights and remedies
Corporate	Consultation	Compliance

These should not be understood as full-fledged doctrines but as ideal-type elements of necessarily composite conceptions of legitimacy. Some actors defend one and only one of these elements – as do the rare purest advocates of national sovereignty or of European federalism – but most actors and scholars refer, explicitly or not, to several of these elements of legitimation. Majone, for example, typically combines technocratic and procedural vectors.

The purpose of this typology is simply to recall that the problem of the Convention is to find a *combination of these vectors that could be acceptable to a quasi-unanimity of its members, and to the largest segments of public opinions.* As scholars, we can argue that the EU is objectively an efficient international organisation, and that as such it is democratic because it is controlled by its member states and because the non-majoritarian institutions they have set up are submitted to strict mechanisms of accountability.[9] However, if this rational argument is not accepted by political leaders and public opinion, because their vision is based on other cognitive and normative frameworks, the EU's democratic legitimacy will remain weak. The contribution the Convention might give to the legitimation of the EU depends on its capacity to reduce the scope and depth of these conflicts of interpretation, by finding a combination of the vectors which is largely acceptable. Theoretically, at least three types of combination can be envisaged.

i) First, the members of the Convention could reach an *ambivalent agreement*, i.e. an agreement on some basic rules based on misunderstanding. The policy preferences of the actors are indeed derived from their fundamental principles and from their beliefs about ends-means relations. In some cases, this can lead to an agreement 'based on preference differences and belief differences that cancel each other';[10] the decision to reject bicameralism in the French *Assemblée constituante* can be understood in these terms.[11] In the EU, the definition of the principle of subsidiarity in the Maastricht Treaty offers an example of this mechanism: some member states thought this principle would limit the growth of EU powers, while others hoped it could be used to launch new policies. Because they disagreed on the 'finality' of the Union and on the likely effect of the principle of subsidiarity, they could agree on the principle itself.

This kind of ambiguous creativity however faces two limits. First, an agreement of this kind is possible on some key elements of a constitutional treaty, but not on the whole text: in some instances, dissonance reduction will clarify the nature of the disagreement and make ambivalent solutions impossible. Secondly, this is always a precarious compromise: the continuous controversy on the extent of the EU's tasks after Maastricht, and the legal/political debate on the nature of the principle of subsidiarity revealed the weakness of the agreement and called for further negotiation.

ii) More often than not, bargaining on the rules of the game will lead to a *modus vivendi* between member states. In Rawls' theory of political constructivism, this is the first step of the process leading to the formation of a well-ordered democratic society.[12] A *modus vivendi* can be forged when the parties realise that there is no other viable solution, though their fundamental principles remain irreconcilable. To illustrate this case, Rawls gives the example of the agreement between Catholics and Protestants on the principle of tolerance in the 16th century: the two opposite camps agreed on this principle, not because they shared moral conceptions of the nature of the individual and of the society, but because they knew that they could not defeat the other party. As soon as the relative strength of one camp would give it a strategic advantage, it would reject the principle. As the agreement did not include a shared perception of the principles on which it was based, it was not stable.

Again, the initial pact between the member states can be seen as a *modus vivendi*. The logic of bargaining produced an aggregation of preferences that was supported by the member states as long as it was coherent with their interest, but challenged when they thought it limited their gains – the crisis of 1965 could be understood in these terms. Given its weakness – its subordination to the circumstances and to the relative strength of the actors – this kind of agreement cannot stabilise a well-ordered society by its own.

iii) Rawls argues that this *modus vivendi* can be the basis of a deeper, larger and more precise agreement – his famous *'overlapping consensus'*. Rawls distinguishes two degrees in this process. First, under certain conditions, a *modus vivendi* can be gradually transformed into a 'constitutional consensus':[13] this occurs when the parties agree on some democratic procedures to solve their conflicts, but do not necessarily agree on a shared conception of the citizen and the society. Three conditions are required to reach this kind of consensus according to Rawls: a) a clear definition of the basic rights and freedoms, which places them beyond political conflict; b) the acceptance of a form of public reason, coherent with the common sense, and necessary to apply these principles; c) the rise of co-operative virtues in politics – such as the sense of moderation and equity, and the spirit of compromise – which are themselves encouraged by the existence of the institutions and their practice. In a second stage, an overlapping consensus can be built on this basis:[14] acting in this framework, the parties tend to modify their comprehensive doctrines under the effect of a practice channelled by the constitutional consensus. The political practice, based on this proceduralised discussion, will gradually strengthen the consensus. It will become deeper (encapsulating a political conception of justice), larger (defining basic laws guaranteeing these principles), and more precise (narrowing the range of liberal conceptions defended by the citizens). All this should, through political co-operation, strengthen the sense of trust on which the society is based.

Given the absence of strong mechanisms of interpersonal and international solidarity in the EU, it cannot be seen as a society based on a Rawlsian 'overlapping consensus'. It is not even sure that its basic treaties can be described as a 'constitutional consensus'. Some could argue that the European Union had already reached this procedural consensus before the creation of the Convention. The adoption of the Charter of Fundamental Rights in December 2000 responds to Rawls' first condition; in a sense, the long practice of co-operation has produced key elements of a common language, and of co-operative behaviour. One could also say, however, that the creation of this body by the Heads of

State and Government bears witness to the fact that they acknowledged the limits of the existing consensus. Their discourse on the method of the Convention is based on the argument that intergovernmental bargaining is, by its very nature, unable to go beyond a *modus vivendi* – or an imperfect constitutional contract; the *raison d'être* of the Convention, as stated by its creators, is specifically to reach a deeper, larger and more precise agreement.

The process : (moderate) Kantian optimism

To what extent should a constitution strengthen the consensus, and how far should it preserve the conflicts which are the basis of democratic politics? This question cannot be given a straightforward answer in constitutional theory.[15] Rawls argues that an overlapping consensus is necessary. But Habermas finds this kind of agreement too weak and too fragile: if the members only agree on the rules, but continue to disagree on the foundations of these rules, the constitution lacks a common understanding and remains subject to permanent divisions. However, the two authors agree on at least one core principle: the consensus must be built through public deliberation, not through secret bargaining.

The analytical (and normative) distinction between the deliberative and bargaining modes of conflict-resolution has become very fashionable in political science in the last ten years. Very schematically, this distinction can be summarised in these terms:

i) *bargaining* is usually defined, in the widely accepted terms of social choice theory, as a process between a) actors with stable preferences, b) who try to maximise their benefits, c) through exchanges of concessions.

ii) by contrast, the advocates of *deliberation* argue that this process takes place among a) actors who are ready to change their preferences, b) when they are convinced by rational arguments, c) in order to reach 'common goods'.[16]

This distinction is based on both analytical and normative grounds. From an analytical point of view, the advocates of deliberation assume that the outcome of the process may be explained by its rules and by the non-utilitarian aims of the actors. From a normative point of view, inspired by neo-Kantian perspectives, this praxis is said to be superior to negotiation. In terms of efficiency, it is supposed to produce 'integrative' results which go beyond the smallest common denominator. In terms of legitimacy, it pretends to build more solid and better accepted solutions. After having argued, the actors not only agree on a norm but also on its justification.[17] Those who have not won at least have the satisfaction of having been heard, and do know why they have lost. The foundations of the agreement being clearer, later conflicts on the basic norms are less likely to occur. Moreover, if deliberation takes place in an open forum, ordinary citizens are given the opportunity to understand the *raison d'être* of the norms, and should therefore accept them more easily.[18] For these reasons, constitutional assemblies are often described as privileged sites of deliberation.[19]

It is difficult, when looking at the European Convention, not to notice that its creators and its members are deeply imbued with such an idealised definition of deliberation.

i) The reasons given by those who advocated the *creation* of this preparatory body clearly refer to this opposition. The classic argument – that can be found in the EP's report, in the Commission's positions, in the discourses of the Belgian Presidency and its Benelux partners – is based on the contrast between the inefficiency and lack of legitimacy of the IGC method, illustrated by the Nice Summit, and the promises of a broader and more open Convention – of which the first Convention gave an example;

ii) The *mandate* defined by the Heads of State and Governments in the Laeken Declaration incorporates some basic elements of a 'deliberative setting'.[20] True, the fact that the Convention will be followed by a classic IGC, and that during its works it will be influenced by the governments from inside – through their representatives – and from outside – through the dialogue between its Chairman and the European Council – confirms that the praxis of bargaining remains crucial.[21] But the deliberative potential of the mandate defined at Laeken should not be neglected. First, the publicity of the debates could force the governments to justify publicly their positions[22] – some of them may have thought that this would actually give them the opportunity to demonstrate that their traditional reluctance is not based on a narrow defence of national interests or on prejudices, but on pragmatic reasoning. Second, as all member states have been given the same number of representatives, it would be very difficult, if not impossible, to vote in such an assembly: in the absence of a system of weighted votes, a majority could represent a very small minority of the European population. The Convention was thus condemned to agree by consensus, rendering the use of vetoes, blocking minorities or winning coalitions very difficult. This, in turn, could preserve the fluidity of the assembly and, without preventing it, limit the resurgence of practices of bargaining. Finally, the fluidity of the body is also encouraged by its mixed composition: in an assembly composed of representatives of the national governments and parliaments – including those of the candidate countries – as well as MEPs and members of the Commission, the classic dividing lines of intergovernmental negotiations could be overcome by new, more flexible and unforeseen coalitions. All this had been, moreover, illustrated by the experience of the Convention that had written the Charter of Fundamental Rights;[23] governments could not say they were unaware of these potential effects of the rules they had defined. And they knew that all Conventions, in the history of modern politics, have always escaped their creators.

iii) The *discourse of the conventionnels* pays tribute to this 'deliberative spirit'. Just to take one example, in his introductory speech, President Giscard invited the members to 'embark on our task without preconceived ideas, and form our vision of the new Europe by listening constantly and closely to all our partners'. Taking this further, he added that 'the members of the four components of our Convention must not regard themselves simply as spokespersons for those who appointed them' and that even if each member would remain 'loyal to his or her brief', he or she also had to 'make his or her personal contribution'.[24] This is, he argued, the key of the 'Convention spirit'. Paraphrasing the ideal-type definition of deliberation, he concluded: 'If your contributions genuinely seek to prepare a consensus, and if you take account of the proposals and comments made by the other members of the Convention, then the content of the final consensus can be worked out step by step here within the Convention'. This, he added, is the crucial difference between the Convention and a classic IGC, which he defined as 'an arena for diplomatic negotiations between member states in which each party sought legitimately to maximise its gains without regard for the overall picture',[25] paraphrasing, this time, the classic definition of bargaining.[26] Giscard's rhetoric is not an isolated example. Most members of the Convention, and the members of the European Council themselves, have underlined these 'promises' of deliberation in their comments on the Convention method.

The weight of this 'deliberative ideal' is important in terms of democratic legitimacy. Whatever may be the result of the Convention, it confirms that, in this phase of European integration dominated by discussions on the institutional framework rather than on the policies of the Union, ideas and ideologies become ever more important.[27] Setting up the Convention was, in itself, a strategy of democratic legitimation, and this is probably one of the reasons why those countries who were not enthusiastic about this idea nevertheless accepted it.[28]

True, the creation of the Convention does not guarantee, in itself, that an answer will be given to the 'democratic challenge facing Europe'. On the contrary, if it did not manage to produce a text widely accepted and understood as 'more democratic' than the former treaties, it would deepen the EU's democratic deficit.[29] The question is thus: will the process matter? Will the Convention be able to produce a 'constitutional consensus' that will stabilise the Union? Will citizens find it more legitimate because it was written by a deliberative body?

This kind of questions cannot be given satisfying empirical answers. First, because we will never know what the outcome of the IGC would have been if the Convention had not existed, and it will be very difficult to demonstrate that the final compromise was forged through deliberations rather than through the negotiations between Heads of State and Government taking place in parallel. Moreover, it cannot be excluded that, within an IGC, actors argue and sometimes alter their preferences after having heard arguments. If this could be demonstrated (and it probably could), this would weaken the analytical distinction between bargaining and deliberation. These methodological biases imply that when the Convention has concluded its work, we will be able to compare its outcome to the status quo ante, but not to compare deliberative and bargaining processes. Secondly, it is nearly impossible to assert when and how the actors changed their mind because of the arguments put forward in the deliberative process. Finally, measuring the changes of perceptions in public opinion requires sophisticated methodologies which are subject to many biases.[30]

Examining the work of the Convention, we could argue that, in many aspects, deliberation works. Its members are organised in political groups, components and sometimes national delegations, but they rarely state it. As they try to combine these three forms of membership, they tend to escape constraints: to be a 'good liberal' one may have to abandon the 'British line'; as an MEP, a Conservative *conventionnel* can have an opinion which is remote from the official line of the Conservative party, and so on. In other terms, 'multiple constraints' can strengthen the autonomy of the actors, who can use a constraint as a pretext for escaping another constraint. Moreover, the complexity of the Convention is such that, as a body, it is much more fluid than an IGC. Agreements are built on oscillating and composite coalitions between a large number of small factions, and we have known since Madison that this weakens the veto of the larger factions. Publicity is also important in the Convention. Even if the members negotiate outside the Convention, their compromise can only be endorsed by the Convention after it has been publicly debated. Some members have strengthened the role of the plenaries, when they used them to announce and explain a shift in the position of their government – as Peter Hain did when he said 'he' (meaning Blair's government) was ready to accept the incorporation of the Charter of Fundamental Rights in the Treaty.

At this stage of the Convention, however, it remains difficult if not impossible to draw definite conclusions. We are condemned to hypothesis and general remarks. I first would like to underline a *paradox of deliberation* which, as far as I know, has not been clearly analysed by theorists of deliberation. This paradox concerns the relation between the two promises of deliberation. On the one hand, this practice is said to be more efficient than bargaining, because it produces dissonance reduction and mutual understanding, and legitimises the attitude of those who change their mind, so that its outcome can be superior to the smallest common denominator. In practice, these dynamics are facilitated by the formation, among the actors of deliberation, of a 'common language' and shared cognitive and normative frameworks. The European Convention illustrates this phenomenon. After a period of 'listening' dominated by vague rhetoric, the *conventionnels* have opted for pragmatic reasoning,[31] and moulded their arguments around the legal and technical terms of the eurojargon. This might help them reach a consensus, as conflicts based on misunderstanding and passions are reduced.[32] But this also tends to weaken the 'external promise' of deliberation. When debates are cast in technical terms, deprived of passionate rhetoric and remote from the citizen's common sense, they do not draw the attention of the general public and do not help citizens understand the issues at stake. The fact that the Convention has been largely ignored by the European press, and the absence of public debate outside the small circles of 'Europeanised' citizens – not to mention the comedy of the 'Forum' – are clear illustrations of the limit placed on this 'public' deliberation.

The consequences of this agreement in terms of democratic legitimacy are ambivalent. On the one hand, those who see the EU as a 'regulatory power' which does not interfere with the functions of the national welfare states might be satisfied by this clarification. The EU will not itself pass and implement legislation guaranteeing a 'certain level of material and social welfare, formation and education'[37] without which people can not participate as citizens. But it does not prevent member states from passing such legislation, if the impact of European norms of competition on social policies is limited, and if the competition between national regimes is softened through flexible co-ordination.[38] In a multi-level polity, all the conditions of a 'well-ordered society' must not necessarily be dealt with at the highest level.

Two objections, however, can be raised against this argument. First, if the EU does not deliver policies related to the citizen's highest expectations, it will remain an abstract level of power. In the absence of mechanisms of interpersonal and international solidarity, a communitarian critique would argue, the sense of belonging will remain weak and the sense of trust fragile. The 'republican' critique of liberal constitutionalism is notably based on the belief that citizens cannot adhere to political principles detached from a thick identity, which itself requires elements of solidarity between social groups.[39] Secondly, in the absence of fiscal and social policies, it remains difficult to politicise European issues.[40] This, in turn, implies that citizens will not be encouraged to participate in EU politics,[41] and that the political principles will remain poorly rooted in their perceptions because they will not be 'personally experienced'.

The Convention does not seem to be willing to transform the *procedures and institutional balances* of the EU either. The permanent opposition between the partisans of a primarily intergovernmental Union and the advocates of the mixed Community model is likely to lead to an 'improved status quo'. If the Franco-German 'compromise' supporting a dual presidency were accepted, it would strengthen the duality of the Union, and probably deepen the conflict between the two sources of legitimacy embodied by the Council and the Commission. But even if a more integrative compromise could be reached – such as a double-hatted Presidency, invested by the European Council and the EP, and chairing the Council and the Commission – it would not fundamentally alter the institutional balance. Such a

President would still be condemned to form ad hoc and complex coalitions of interests in the Council and the EP. The EU would remain, in other words, a 'power-sharing' democracy, characterised by a deep division of the 'society' and a strong ethos of consensus.[42]

Limited to a regulatory power and a framework of co-ordination, and remaining a complex institutional system based on variable coalitions, the EU is likely to be perceived as an abstract and remote level of power. This, Tocqueville argued, is the fate of federalism:

> 'The Union is a vast body, which presents no definite object to patriotic feeling. The forms and limits of the state are distinct and circumscribed, since it represents a certain number of objects that are familiar to the citizens and dear to them all. It is identified with the soil; with the right of property and the domestic affections; with the recollections of the past, the labors of the present, and the hopes of the future. Patriotism, then, which is frequently a mere extension of individual selfishness, is still directed to the state and has not passed over to the Union. Thus the tendency of the interests, the habits, and the feelings of the people is to center political activity in the states in preference to the Union.'[43]

Coming back to Bush Jr's USA, Tocqueville would probably recognise that he had underestimated the force of the Union. Looking at the EU, we should not proclaim the end of history too fast. In the long term, the perspective of a centralisation of power and of a clearer polarisation of issues – two elements of a liberal democracy generally considered by political scientists as vectors of civic consciousness[44] – cannot be excluded. The 'regulatory' issues are not immune to conflicts. The European party federations already have different visions of how the single market should be regulated, and these divisions do not substantially differ from the classic European left-right cleavage. Questions related to internal security – and freedoms – generate a form of political polarisation which also follows the lines of the left-right opposition. Political practice could strengthen these reference points and simplify the 'political offer'. In parallel, the generalisation of codecision in legislative areas could clarify the function of the Commission vis-à-vis the EP and the Council. A German-like evolution remains theoretically possible in the long term. These, however, are fragile prospects. In the foreseeable future, the EU is likely to remain a form of 'deliberative polyarchy'.[45] As such, it can be seen as a satisfying democratic polity by those who share the assumptions of a strictly liberal democracy. But those who support a more ambitious version of democracy – which does not renounce the Millian ideal of civic education – will continue to criticise its lack of ambition.[46]

Some (provisional) conclusions

These two debates – on distributive justice and on civic participation – do not necessarily undermine the EU's democratic legitimacy. The existence of a permanent discussion on the constitutional principles is often seen as an essential element of any liberal democracy.[47] The question, in today's Europe, is this: has the EU reached this balance between consensus and conflict on the foundations which is the substance of democratic legitimacy? And is the Convention likely to contribute to it?

The impact of the Convention should not be overestimated. *Pace* the nostalgic defenders of a United States of Europe, the *conventionnels* are not likely to make a 'révolution des pouvoirs', and they do not contemplate a European 'New Deal'. The Union of states they are trying to redefine will remain very different from Westminster democracies and from European welfare states. Seen from a 'republican' point of view – even a moderate republicanism such as that of Habermas – this Union will be unable to build 'democratic legitimacy', because it will always lack the comprehensive doctrines, the sense of belonging and pride that are supposed to be the foundations of contemporary democracies. Citizens will not die for the Union. They will not even pay taxes for it.

The contribution of the Convention should not, however, be underestimated. Analysed through less exacting standards – which are probably more coherent with the preferences of largely depoliticised citizens – the Union might be seen as a democratically legitimate polity. The Convention could help strengthen this argument. First and foremost because of its method. Since it represents, relatively well,[48] the diversity of European opinion, and is composed of many ordinary representatives who had no clear opinion on the Union before becoming members of this assembly, and since all questions were on the table and discussed publicly, it will be more difficult to argue that its outcome was not really accepted. The ratification of the treaty will probably be the key of the process. The attitude of the minority will be important here: if the most federalist and sovereignist minorities continue to criticise the agreement after a 'consensus' – which, in Giscard's terms 'does not mean unanimity' – has been reached, this will undermine the text; on the other hand, if they acknowledge that their point of view was defeated by a very large majority, after they had been given the opportunity to make their point, the consensus will be strengthened. The quality of the deliberation, and the satisfaction it provides to its actors, might determine their attitude. The kind of argument used by those who will support the new treaty will be very important too. If they argue that 'the treaty is good because it supports our interests' this will not strengthen the foundations of the agreement. If, on the contrary, they explain that the treaty is the best possible compromise between still largely different interests and visions, this might help citizens understand the nature of the agreement. The legitimacy of the Union would be strengthened, not because its capacities would be developed, but because the expectations of the citizens, who would understand the nature of the EU better, would be reduced.

Finally, the impact of forms should not be underestimated either. If the Convention manages to write a simple, clear and understandable text, the consensus might grow.[49] Western minds are forged by formal categories, and the conformity of the Union's basic text to the canons of Western law would make it more acceptable.[50] Giscard is probably right when he says that words matter. If the *conventionnels* were able to find formulas to explain that the Union is less than a state but more than a confederation, this could help dissipate the phantasms of those who still fear, or contemplate, the construction of a European state.

The Convention is not reinventing the European Union. More modestly, its members try to reappraise and rephrase it. In the American history, the Constitution was the outcome of a long debate on the vices and virtues of federalism and sovereignty. In the EU, the Constitution came first, through piecemeal instrumental arrangements and without debate. The EU is now experiencing this debate, *ex post facto*. Even if it only confirms the agreement, this might make it more solid.

Notes

[1] A first version of this paper was presented at a Conference organised by the Minda de Gunzburg Center for European Studies, Harvard University, 31 January 2003. I would like to thank the participants for their very helpful comments, and particularly Peter Hall, Jane Jenson, Andy Moravcsik, George Ross, Fritz Scharpf, Vivien Schmidt and David Trubek.

[2] Craig, 1999.

[3] This section is based on Lord and Magnette, 2000.

[4] Habermas, 2001.

[5] Majone, 1996.

[6] Majone, 2001.

[7] Magnette, 2003.

[8] Scharpf, 1998.

[9] Moravcsik, 2002.

[10] Elster, 1998.

[11] Elster, 1994.

[12] Rawls, 1993. IV, §3.

[13] Ibid. IV, § 6.

[14] Ibid. IV, § 7.

[15] Sunstein, 2001.

[16] Elster, 1998; Dryzek, 2000.

[17] Habermas, 1996.

[18] Manin, 1998.

[19] Elster, 1998.

[20] Elster, 1998.

[21] The geographic and political balance of the Praesidium also corresponds to a classic intergovernmental logic. The fact that the Secretariat of the Convention is provided by the General Secretariat of the Council is another sign of this classic pattern.

The non-decisional nature of the Convention is neatly affirmed in the Laeken Declaration: the text says that 'it will be the task of that Convention to *consider* the key issues arising for the Union's future development and try to *identify the various possible options*'; the final document is said to 'provide a *starting point* for discussions in the Intergovernmental Conference, which will take the ultimate decisions' (emphasis added).

[22] Theories of deliberation show that the principle of publicity can have perverse effects, in that the actors may be tempted to use rhetoric to convince the external audience (Elster 1998). But this does not occur in a Convention which is largely ignored by the general public.

[23] Braibant, 2001; Deloche-Gaudez, 2001.

[24] Inaugural speech: 8 and 13. He added during a press conference that the term 'representative' was a 'erreur de rédaction' since 'ce ne sont pas des représentants, lorsqu'ils parlent, ils ne disent pas parler au nom de l'une ou l'autre composante', *Agence Europe*, 28 March 2002: 6. Jose María Aznar, as President of the European Council had on the contrary argued that the members had to follow the views of the organs they represented. In his speech to the inaugural session, Aznar however insisted on the virtues

of deliberation, on behalf of the European Council: transmitting the opinion of the quasi-unanimity of the members of the European Council, he argued that 'Nice is the reason why we are here today.' Partly re-writing the history, he added that 'Immediately thereafter, the Heads of State and Governments convened the Convention that is starting now, in the knowledge that *the new stage calls for new forms of operation and deliberation* in order to continue to create 'more Europe'' (emphasis added).

[23] Speech: 13. In the same vein, see his opinion published by *Le Monde* on 23 July 2002: 'Il ne s'agit pas de rouvrir, de manière précipitée, d'anciens débats, comme la querelle entre fédéralistes et intergouvernementalistes, ou la rivalité entre la Commission et le Conseil, qui se sont brisés sur les écueils d'Amsterdam et de Nice, mais de faire avancer le groupe pour vérifier s'il peut découvrir, en fin de parcours, une solution globale commune.'

[24] In a press conference after the session of 22 March, Giscard said he found it 'normal que les grandes sensibilités européennes harmonisent leurs points de vue' while however warning against any 'structuration excessive' of the Convention, *Agence Europe*, 23 March 2002: 12. On 12 July, after many members had presented their argument as their state's position, he recalled 'qu'il ne s'agira pas de s'exprimer d'un point de vue national (…). Nous attendons des conventionnels une expression européenne'.

In his opinion published by *Le Monde* on 23 July 2002, he said about the representatives of the governments: 'Leur situation comporte une certaine ambiguïté: participent-ils en tant que personne aux travaux et aux interrogations de la Convention, ou viennent-ils y exprimer le point de vue des gouvernements qui les ont désignés? Après un premier flottement, il m'a semblé que leur caractère de 'conventionnel' s'affirmait'.

[25] Moravcsik and Nicolaïdis, 1998.

[26] It remains difficult to assert why Britain and Denmark, who had been surprised and annoyed by the first Convention, have accepted this process. One hypothesis is that the Belgian Presidency, presenting this initiative as one element of a broader debate, reduced its importance and made it acceptable. But the representatives of these member states were probably not so naïve – and if they were, they will not acknowledge this in interviews. Another hypothesis is that these countries found it difficult to refuse a Convention and thought it more efficient to try and control it – hence their strategy to amend the Laeken Declaration and open new questions, their insistence on the non-decisional nature of this body and their willingness to integrate candidate countries, supposed to be less prone to support further integration. If this hypothesis is right, as I believe it is, it means that these countries acknowledged the need to set up a process inspired by a democratic constitutional tradition.

[27] From a formal point of view, as its members were not explicitly elected by the citizens of the member states to write a European constitution, the Convention remains less democratic than a national constitutional assembly.

[28] In Fishkin's experiences, the same sample is questioned before and after the deliberative process to measure this change (Fishkin, 1995). Given that, as far as I know, no systematic polls were made before the Convention on these issues, comparison will be difficult: moreover, Eurobarometers are often criticised for not being immune to misinterpretations due to cultural diversity and the small size of the samples.

[29] A pragmatic constitutional reasoning is based on reasoning on the likely effect of norms. Sartori opposes this deliberative style to the 'rationalist' style based on conceptual reasoning and to the empiricist style founded on the lessons of historical experience (Sartori, 1965). According to Sartori, the first case is typical of American constitutionalism, while the second is illustrated by the French and the third by the British history.

[30] Perelman and Olbrechts-Tyteca, 1969.

[31] Bohman, 1996: 241.

[32] Though, in this case, the argument on the deliberation by some of its actors was more important than the deliberation itself.

[35] Sunstein, 2001.

[36] The ' explanations' of the rights of the Charter, written by the Praesidium in order to explain their meaning (and thereby limit the margins of judicial interpretation) were a crucial element in reaching a consensus. In the new Convention, several members have asked for the incoporation of these 'explanations' in the new treaty. This illustrates the impact of deliberation, and its 'rational outcome' to build and strengthen consensus.

[37] Rawls 1993: IV, § 6,3.

[38] Scharpf, 1998

[39] Habermas, 2001.

[40] Moravcsik, 2002.

[41] Magnette, 2003.

[42] Lijphart, 1999.

[43] de Tocqueville, 1889: Chapter XVIII.

[44] Przeworski, Manin and Stokes, 1999.

[45] Gerstenberg and Sabel, 2002.

[46] Habermas, 1996; 2001.

[47] Aron, 1968; Lefort, 1988; Habermas, 1996; Sunstein, 2001.

[48] Given the decentralised mechanism of selection of the members, the parties which are on the left and right-wing extremes of national arenas are underrepresented in the Convention – there was only one Green representative before Mr Fischer's entry.

[49] Rawls notes that 'constitutional essentials' must not be too detailed and that their principles must be 'made visible' in the institutions in order to benefit from a large support (Rawls, 1993 : VI, §6, 1).

[50] Weiler, 1999.

What's in a Convention? Process and substance in the project of European constitution-building

Jo Shaw

Introduction

Since its creation was first announced in December 2001 at the Laeken European Council meeting, very substantial expectations have been invested in the Convention on the Future of the Union by many observers of the European integration process. Perhaps it could finally address the yawning legitimacy gap that appears to have opened up in European public affairs since the time of the Treaty of Maastricht, leading to a widespread alienation between the activities of the European institutions and those whom they are meant – like any public bodies – to serve, that is, the citizens and residents of the member states. Of course, bridging the legitimacy gap was only one of the ideas motivating those responsible for establishing the Convention. It was additionally supposed to engage discussion amongst a wider range of elites on questions of reform than had hitherto been achieved in the context of intergovernmental conferences ('IGCs') and to deal with a number of intractable problems, especially those related to institutional reform in the context of enlargement, the solution of which had eluded the negotiators in the IGCs of 1996-97 and 2000.

While it was never likely to be a panacea for all the (real and imagined) evils of European Union ('EU' or 'Union'), the Convention quickly began to engage, with an intensity never before seen in a European institution, with practical questions about the establishment of a formal constitutional foundation for the EU. The Laeken mandate for the Convention contained in fact little direct focus on the constitutional question, but provided instead a general analysis of the 'state' of the European integration process and the challenges it faces, harked back in particular to the four issues (competences, status of the Charter of Fundamental Rights, simplification of the treaties and the role of national parliaments) articulated in the Declaration No. 23 on the Future of the Union appended to the Treaty of Nice in December 2000, and set out many questions – some fifty-six – which it saw as underpinning the diagnosis. What the Laeken Declaration did provide – for the first time ever in a document endorsed by all the Heads of State and Government of the EU's member states – was a specific reference to the 'C' word, in a passage contemplating a trajectory 'Towards a Constitution for European citizens'. The discussion in the text is specifically linked to the question of simplification and reorganisation, changes which are assumed to be linked in turn to the goal of transparency. The Declaration then asks:

> 'whether this simplification and reorganisation might not lead in the long run to the adoption of a constitutional text in the Union. What might the basic features of such a constitution be? The values which the Union cherishes, the fundamental rights and obligations of its citizens, the relationship between the member states and the Union?'

These issues and more have preoccupied the Convention's work. In certain respects, its work has been the logical continuation of previous efforts to articulate a formal constitutional framework for the European integration process, efforts to which the European Parliament in particular has contributed in a very substantial way, especially through its 1984 Draft Treaty on European Union. To that extent, it is hardly surprising that the Laeken Declaration is not always treated as an authoritative source of inspiration and legitimacy for the Convention, since the Convention projects itself as having an even wider and grander vision which is not restricted by the already wide-ranging analysis offered by Laeken. As Andrew Duff, ELDR MEP and member of the Convention, rather dramatically declared in a mid-Convention interview, 'Nobody reads the Laeken Declaration any longer'.[1]

A different sort of bigger picture is offered in this chapter. By no means does the Convention operate against the background of a constitutional *tabula rasa* in relation to either the process of constitution-building or the substantive constitutional choices which it is making. The treaties and indeed the Union's own Charter of Fundamental Rights proclaimed in declaratory form in 2000 are not the only sources of constitutional *acquis* which the Convention must grapple with in developing the text which its President plans to send on to the European Council when it concludes its deliberations. Constitution-building in the EU since the inception of the first treaties has comprised a set of complex interactions and tensions between the treaty texts and other formal institutional documents, on the one hand, and their interpretation by key actors, notably the Court of Justice, but also the national courts, and the other non-judicial EU institutions, on the other. This has been characterised as a distinction between the 'formal' and 'real' constitutions of the EU.[2]

These interactions and tensions map onto both the procedural and substantive dimensions of the Convention's work. For example, in relation to procedural questions such as 'how, when and where does constitutional development of the EU take place?', it is clear that constitutional development occurs in a number of overlapping forums, such as intergovernmental conferences, national ratification processes for new treaties (which have included some key national constitutional court judgements[3]), and subsequent interpretations and applications of the treaties by the Court of Justice and other institutional actors. The question which this chapter considers is how the Convention has added to the process of the development of the *acquis* through its working methods and through the management of the process by key actors such as President Giscard d'Estaing. In relation to the substantive content of the current European constitutional framework, the general principles of law articulated by the Court of Justice via its jurisdiction founded on Article 220 of the Treaty establishing the European Community ('EC') are often as important as the specific treaty texts, although the Court did announce in the 1986 case of *Les Verts*[4] that the EC Treaty can be characterised as the Community's constitutional charter.[5] Furthermore, there are many key texts of a political nature, such as the Charter of Rights, a number of interinstitutional agreements on matters such as the budget or the operation of the legislative procedure, as well as legislation of a quasi-constitutional character such as the rules on the electoral procedure for the European Parliament, which are not contained in the formal text of the treaties, but which one might very well expect to be encapsulated somewhere in a formal constitutional structure, perhaps in an annex or protocol, if not indeed (as should be the case with the Charter) in the main body of the Constitution itself. Overall, the Court's so-called 'constitutionalisation' of the original Treaty of Rome to incorporate federal legal features such as the supremacy of European Community ('EC') law over national law, the penetration of EC law into the national legal orders, and the existence of various mechanisms, notably direct effect, whereby individuals have been able to enforce their EC law rights in national courts against member states, represents more of an elaboration of constitutional principles based on a reading of the 'spirit' of the original treaties than it does a direct derivation from the texts as agreed by the High Contracting Parties either in 1957 or subsequently. This chapter looks at the use of this *acquis* in the context of the development of the text of a Constitutional Treaty.

In sum, the main objective of this chapter is to elaborate in more detail the ways in which the Convention's work is structured by the complex procedural and substantive heritage of the Union's constitutional *acquis*. Procedural perspectives on the Convention have focused on the ways in which the Convention supplements the existing constitutionalisation processes of the European Union, for example, by adding an additional 'pre-contractual' phase to the process whereby member states already agree upon changes to the international treaties which remain the formal construct of European integration[6] and by introducing the notion of consensus amongst elites as the basis for 'agreeing' a new constitutional settlement. At the very least, the constitutional dialogues which shape the EU are immeasurably enriched by the complex constellations of interest intermediation which the Convention comprises via its plenary debates, working groups, and discussion circles, and in its draft texts and amendments. Furthermore, in more or less open ways, the Convention and its members are in constant dialogue with external interests, such as national parliaments, other European institutions, civil society and even academia. The Convention offers as a minimum the promise of deliberation, and perhaps a great deal more than that. In the future, it is even arguable that the application of the Convention method could lead to a comprehensive redesign of the constitutional amendment process and the eventual abandonment of traditional international law methods of treaty amendment. But that would be to assume a constitutional revolution which lies some way in the future. Shorter term, it is possible to envisage some type of halfway house involving the abandonment of the requirement of unanimity for the entry into force of treaty amendments, but this may need to be on the basis that non-consenting states are not themselves bound but move into a state of association with the Union. While this chapter associates itself in large measure with the arguments presented in this volume by Paul Magnette and Lars Hoffmann, it also picks up in Section 3 one specific procedural question namely the emergence of a distinctive Convention *acquis* and the question of how this sits with the wider Union *acquis* in the constitutional sphere.[7]

Shifting the focus to substantive questions (Section 4), the chapter shows that the Convention is forcing political actors at the national and European levels to confront more directly than ever before some key questions. To what extent do they wish the realities of European constitutionalism (such as the principle of the supremacy of EU law) to remain hidden from public view in the future as in many respects they have done hitherto? And can the delicate balance of the national and the supranational dimensions of European integration (not to mention the subnational and international inputs which it experiences) survive the sometimes harsh scrutiny to which it is now being subjected within the confines of the Convention process?

To set the scene for this discussion, the next section provides a preliminary sketch and synopsis of the evolution of the EU constitutional framework from the inception of the first treaties until the present time. The objective of this section is to show that notwithstanding the late arrival of the European Council and many of the member state governments at the 'constitutional party', the idea of analysing European integration in constitutionalist terms has been well-established for decades. While the practice has been particularly common amongst lawyers, it has also extended to both students and practitioners of politics.[8] At the same time, however, the constitutional question remains highly contested in relation to the innumerable sub-questions which it encapsulates, including the very purpose and scope of a constitution for an entity such as the EU which is not formally a state in the Westphalian sense, albeit that it wields many instruments and undertakes many tasks of a state-like nature. On the contrary, it operates in some sort of ambiguous liminal space between states and international organisations according to the conventional definitions of national and international law, and it is widely regarded as deserving of analysis primarily as a *sui generis* entity which cannot easily be assimilated to other known forms of political organisation. Above all, however, the very ethic of European constitutionalism remains contested.

A central premise of this chapter is that whatever happens with the Convention, it is important to develop principled reference points for viewing both the evolution of the Convention process and the substantive outcomes which the Convention adopts. Elsewhere I have argued for the importance of a critical assessment of the Convention process, in the light of principles of responsible and inclusive constitutionalism.[9] This chapter has a separate but related objective to link the tensions which frame the procedural dimension of the Convention to some of the key elements of its substantive debate. With that objective in mind, the chapter looks explicitly at the constitutional *acquis* as the background to the constitution-building process, as well as contributing to reflection upon the novelty and *sui generis* nature of the Convention process. That paradox of the rootedness of the Convention's discussions in the constitutional *acquis* at the same time as it proposes sometimes innovative solutions to apparently intractable problems will remain, in my view, one of the most enduring features of the Convention experience.

A brief history and synopsis of constitution-building in the European Union

The current 'constitutional' debate in the European Union is not a dramatic departure in the development of the 'ever closer union', but a continuation of longstanding debates in many academic and some media, opinion-former and political circles about the finality of European integration. Posing the question in constitutional terms is hardly new. The German Government official report attached to the text of the Treaty of Paris establishing the European Coal and Steel Community, which went before the *Bundestag* in 1951 described the system to be established as 'a European model of a constitutional type'.[10] Yet it took nearly fifty years for the term 'constitution' to reach the collective intergovernmental discourse of what is now the European

Union in the form of the Laeken Declaration, and even then it does not acquire a capital 'C' – although it has done so frequently in the context of the Convention's deliberations.

On the long road to Laeken and the Convention, as already mentioned in the introduction, the Court of Justice has made an unrivalled contribution to the reconstruction of the discourse of European integration in juristic terms as a proto-constitutionalist discourse. Although not originally articulated in terms of a formal constitutional framework, the Court's proposition that the European Communities constitute a 'new legal order for the benefit of which states have limited their sovereignty rights, albeit within limited fields, and the subjects of which comprise not only member states but also their nationals'[11] makes it clear that any state which accedes to the European Union is joining something quite different to the United Nations or even the Council of Europe. Indeed, the Court made that very same point in explicit terms: 'The objective of the EEC Treaty, which is to establish a Common Market, the functioning of which is of direct concern to interested parties in the Community, implies that this Treaty is *more than an agreement which merely creates mutual obligations between the contracting States.*'[12] Even so, whatever one makes of the Court's case law on the relationship between what is now widely known as EU law and national law, on the development of the Community's, and later, the Union's own competences and of concepts such as implied powers or the preemption of national legislative competence, on the development of fundamental rights as general principles of EU law, and most recently on the construction of citizenship rights based on the principle of non-discrimination on grounds of nationality, this still remains a relatively fractured constitutional system. It is important not to overstate either the completeness or the coherence of the European Union's current constitutional framework.[13] There are aspects of the existing constitutional law which have escaped logical explanation, such as the operation of the pillar system, which are not well understood, such as the system governing the attribution, exercise and control of competences, or which are generally accepted not to be working particularly well, such as the concept of subsidiarity.[14] Moreover, it is important not to confuse the proposition that the EU has a constitutional framework (probably best designated with small 'c' and small 'f') with the debate about whether Europe *ought* to have a Constitution, with a capital 'C'.

Despite the fears that the institution of the wider, looser European Union by the Treaty of Maastricht would lead to a dilution of the constitutional element of the previous European Communities, because of the intergovernmentalist character of the so-called second and third pillars, in fact there has been an acceleration in the turn to constitutionalism and normative discourse generally since Maastricht.[15] One reason has obviously been the attempt to counteract perceived public disillusionment with the European integration project by offering the idea of a constitution for the European Union, both as an actually existing framework and as a future project for development, as one way of guaranteeing government subject to the rule of law and respect for individual rights against majoritarian tyranny. It is also increasingly widely accepted that it is possible to conceive of the European Union – despite the diversity of legal arrangements which it encapsulates – as a single constitutional framework, with a single legal order. Amongst the most important factors linking right across the Union's system are the common principles and values, especially those contained in Article 6(1) of the Treaty on European Union (liberty, democracy, respect for human rights and fundamental freedoms, and the rule of law).[16] It is no surprise that the debate over values and principles has been central to the Convention's discussion of what constitutes the foundational framework for the European Union.

Not all commentators who argue that the EU already has a constitutional framework necessarily agree that this would be 'improved' as a result of the Convention's intervention. Notably, Joseph Weiler focuses on the risk that a constitution in a formal sense – especially if there were some attempt to depart from the international law basis of the current arrangement and to assert that the EU could be legitimated via popular participation at the present stage of its development – would upset the delicate constitutional balance based on 'tolerance' which he identifies as the basis for the EU at the present stage. He argues that

> 'constitutional actors in the member states accept the European constitutional discipline not because, as a matter of legal doctrine, as is the case in the federal state, they are subordinate to a higher sovereignty and authority attaching to norms validated by the federal people, the constitutional *demos*. They accept it as an autonomous voluntary act, endlessly renewed on each occasion, of subordination, in the discrete areas governed by Europe to a norm which is the aggregate expression of other wills, other political identities, other political communities.'[17]

The resistance to the allures of the formal constitution makes Weiler, it would seem, something close to a constitutional absolutist or purist, restricting the ascription of 'true constitution' to a limited range of incidents of 'polity-hood' which satisfy certain conditions of process and substance generally associated most readily with states. In other words, states have an inbuilt advantage in terms of their need for, and receptiveness of, formal constitutional frameworks which link political power to a constitutional *demos*, or *pouvoir constituant*. This is the field of legitimacy claims in which the European Union continues to struggle, notwithstanding the institution of concepts such as European citizenship, or the establishment of a system of direct elections to the European Parliament and the investiture of greater powers in that directly elected body.

Even for those convinced by the argument that a certain degree of constitutional formalism can offer legitimacy gains to a struggling European Union, in both the shorter and the longer terms, the complex history of constitution-building in the EU sketched here counsels against hasty conclusions about the impact of the Convention in relation to issues of either process or substance. Yet the tenor of President Giscard d'Estaing's first speech to the opening session of the Convention on 28 February 2002 set out very clearly his belief in the constitutive power and capacity of the Convention. Mentioning the word 'constitution' three times, he then concluded with a powerful attempt to preempt much debate by declaring the aim of the Convention thus:

> 'The Laeken Declaration leaves the Convention free to choose between submitting options or making a single recommendation. It would be contrary to the logic of our approach to choose now. However, there is no doubt that, in the eyes of the public, our recommendation would carry considerable weight and authority *if we could manage to achieve broad consensus on a single proposal which we could all present*. If we were to reach consensus on this point, *we would thus open the way towards a Constitution for Europe*. In order to avoid any disagreement over semantics, let us agree now to call it: a 'constitutional treaty for Europe'.'[18] (emphasis in the original)

It is difficult to imagine a more effective presentation of the historical opportunity which Giscard saw the Convention as offering – an opportunity which he might have seen in a certain sense as being for himself as an individual, but which he effectively portrayed to the new

Convention as a collective opportunity. This sense of opportunity in turn spoke eloquently to the federalist majority amongst the Convention members, and so the endeavour has become Giscard's main 'gift' to the Convention, which means that despite subsequent tensions, his leadership still retained a substantial element of goodwill amongst the ordinary Convention members, at least until the row over the articles on the institutions in April 2003.

Even so, part way through the process, it remained impossible to predict whether the Convention would succeed in pre-empting the subsequent IGC charged with formal treaty amendment in any substantial respect, although clear evidence emerged from the very beginning of the Convention's deliberation that it might well have a (surprisingly powerful) capacity to lock in the member states and to constrain their freedom of action in the IGC. Perhaps more crucially, in terms of the acceptability and legitimacy of any constitutional settlement coming out of this process, there is no strong evidence that the involvement of a wider range of elite actors in constitutional debate is necessarily going to facilitate the process of securing acceptance and therefore ratification by referendum or parliamentary assent *within* the member states, *after* the IGC.[19] Moreover, a Convention charged most obviously with the task of overcoming long-standing blockages to reform of the 'old' European Community institutions and with simplifying the mind-boggling complexities of the European Union's architectural structure has found how often these are themselves hedged around by the Court of Justice's constitutionalising endeavours, in relation to issues such as rights, competences, the effects of EU law, and 'interinstitutional balance'. A 'simple' common sense prescription of constitutional fundamentals and of principles of legitimate political leadership was always likely to elude the grasp of the Convention members, however long they laboured. The proposition which this chapter pursues is that unravelling the blend of the old and the new in the process and substance of the Convention's work is a necessary precondition to making an assessment of its contribution to working towards a European Constitution. This approach is in line with my earlier argument not to develop *a priori* assumptions about whether the Convention is 'good' or 'bad' for the EU's development as a legitimate and effective polity.[20]

The procedural dimension of Convention-watching: the 'building' of the Convention 'acquis'

In other contributions to this volume, Paul Magnette and Lars Hoffmann have addressed aspects of the Convention process, in so far as it offers the opportunity for a deeper and more effective legitimation of the European Union as well as the narrower possibility of changing the long term trajectory of treaty amendment processes (perhaps even into 'purer' constitution-making processes). It would be idle to repeat these points here, but they constitute an important supplementation to the argument about the articulation and deployment of a Convention *acquis* which is the focus in this chapter.

When Convention-watching, it is commonplace to point out that the Convention is clearly more open, more transparent and more inclusive than an IGC, that it 'decides' by 'consensus' and does not incorporate a set of formal veto arrangements, and that it involves a wider range of elites, giving an institutionalised voice to the European Parliament and to national parliaments in the process. These are points which are in some sense both otiose and banal, given that the Convention is a very different beast to the IGC both in terms of purpose and composition.

In fact, formal constitution-building in the European Union is a complex, multi-staged process, already involving an ever increasing range of actors.[21] While the first significant set of amendments to the EEC Treaty – the Single European Act of 1986 – might have occurred away from the glare of all but the most Euro-focussed publicity, subsequent cases of treaty amendment, although often not front-page affairs, have attracted much more substantial media coverage, not least because of the referendum affairs in Denmark (Maastricht) and Ireland (Nice). As things stand, the Convention adds a further 'pre-contractual' stage to the process; it does not – and cannot, at least until the rules of the game are themselves formally changed by treaty amendment – formally pre-empt or replace the Intergovernmental Conference as the site within which formal commitments are made between the member states. The latter remain the legal 'Masters of the Treaty'. On the other hand, so far as the member states are being required to engage in the endeavour to find compromise and consensus positions on key questions about the missions, functions, values and operating procedures and practices of the European Union which have historically been fudged or swept to the sidelines as posing insoluble problems, they are doing so in a very different framework to that of an IGC. In part, they have reacted to that by seeking to make the Convention more like an IGC, as more and more states have nominated foreign ministers or other cabinet rank ministers to be their representatives on the Convention. On the other hand, the change in the environment may enable the Convention and the member states in particular to break away from certain taboos which have constrained their behaviour within IGCs when discussing historical blocking points such as institutional reform and the question of the future of the institutional system designed in the 1950s for a 'Community' of Six, rather than a twenty-first century 'Union' of twenty-five plus. One clearly important innovation, for example, which creates a very different feel to the Convention as compared to the IGC is the presence of national opposition parties through the medium of national parliamentary representatives and European parliamentary representatives, sitting in the same debating chamber and round the same negotiating table as national governmental representatives. This breaks down the sense of the unitary 'national' interest as represented by national governments which has often stifled the development of intergovernmental negotiations and ensured that they predictably remain bargaining rather than deliberation scenarios. Indeed, this change seems to offer the promise of deliberation – if not yet quite the reality, or so the consensus of reports from professional Convention-watchers seems to indicate.[22]

There is one particularly important dimension of the Convention process which contributes directly to the linking of questions of process and substance. This is the question of how the Convention proceeds, especially in the context of its 'endgame' involving the discussion, amendment and agreement of specific treaty provisions, towards putative agreement upon a Constitutional Treaty. How can we understand this endgame? Can we find out its details by looking at the Convention's website?

In fact, within just a few months of the Convention's establishment, there was already an overwhelming body of written material on the Convention website. This effectively precludes the casual visitor to the site from gaining anything more than a very superficial review of what the Convention is and does from the very brief and relatively uninformative introductory materials which the website provides.[23] The website does not explain for the general user how and why the Convention is in fact working towards a new Constitutional Treaty, making reference only briefly to some of the questions in the Laeken Declaration, but omitting any form of articulation of how the Convention agenda and approach shifted in its early months into the constitutional register.[24] Clicking on 'Draft Constitutional Treaty' on the website merely brings up the highly impenetrable skeleton put forward by the Praesidium in October 2002,[25] the rafts of draft articles which have followed since January 2003, and the multitudes of amendments put forward by Convention members. That is the negative side of the Convention and its website, which was quickly turned into a tool which would be useful only to those staying very close to the Convention debate. The positive side of the website lies in that very same mass of material which is impenetrable to the casual visitor, but which can in fact reveal to those who have followed the process from the beginning much of the complexity and richness of the constitution-building process, and the different elements of which it is composed.

This process has involved the creation and deployment for developmental purposes of the Convention's own *acquis*,[26] based on deliberations in Working Groups and plenary, the prefatory, summative and drafting work of the Secretariat including the preparation of working documents and questionnaires, reports, summaries of meetings and draft articles, and the discussions and resolutions of the Praesidium. Not all of these processes and outcomes are equally public. Notably the Praesidium has always deliberated behind closed doors, and, notwithstanding objections,[27] does not produce minutes of its meetings. Working Group meetings, furthermore, were generally not open to public observation, whereas plenary meetings are not only public and televised (and fully linguistically accessible because of simultaneous interpretation), but are also recorded *verbatim* in transcripts on the European Parliament website which will ultimately be available in all official languages.

The analysis of Secretariat documentation – much of which is passed via the Praesidium for approval and adopted as Praesidium documentation, perhaps after amendment – is perhaps the most illuminating exercise in excavating the emergence of the Convention's *acquis*. The Secretariat provides, *inter alia*, the bridge between the Convention and some of the most effective institutional players in the

EU, namely the secretariats and legal services of the Council and the Commission, which have an unparalleled expertise in understanding the present state of EU law as well as a background as repeat players in IGCs over the years. The Convention Secretariat has played an essential role in setting out the richness and variety of the EU's existing constitutional *acquis* by preparing and issuing documentation notes on issues such as the present system of competence distribution and allocation, the legal instruments of the EU, the nature of the open method of co-ordination, the state of play in external action and justice and home affairs, the role of national parliaments and the institutions of the EU, and the regional and local dimension of EU governance. While largely descriptive, these papers have had the capacity also to shape debate because of their effective command of the current *status quo*. Allied to this, the Secretariat has more directly shaped debate by preparing papers on questions such as the possibilities of simplification as envisaged by the Declaration on the Future of the Union and the Laeken Declaration.[28] In that sense, the Secretariat has contributed directly to innovation as well as to explaining the relevance of the EU's constitutional *acquis* to the Convention's own work. Inevitably, of course, the Secretariat will have provided the background expertise for the preparation of crucial documents such as the mandates of the Working Groups and (in almost all cases) the Working Group draft reports, under the political control of the Praesidium and, especially, the Chairs of the respective Working Groups who are in turn drawn from the Praesidium. Likewise, the Secretariat will have provided substantial input for crucial documents such as the October skeleton for a new Constitutional Treaty[29] and the subsequent tranches of draft articles.[30]

Interestingly it is not entirely clear to what extent there have been other, even less visible, influences (perhaps from the team personally assisting Giscard) upon some of those drafts. A good example is the idea of dual citizenship which is not a derivation from the existing treaties, which mysteriously appeared in the skeleton published in October 2002,[31] but which disappeared from the February 2003 draft of Articles 1-16 in favour of a return to the text of the existing EC/EU Treaties.[32] What has been clear has been the Secretariat's role in preparing reports on reactions to the draft articles and beginning the task of collating the huge number of amendments proposed, especially to Articles 1-16, a daunting exercise in the management of information and many competing initiatives.

That comment leads directly to the final aspect of process which needs to be highlighted in this section of the chapter, namely the management of the whole process of constitution-building. When the member states agreed, in the Laeken Declaration, to the establishment of the Convention, one of the 'checks' which they placed upon its capacity to produce unintended, and perhaps unwanted, outcomes was the nomination of ex-French president Giscard d'Estaing to chair the Convention, bearing in mind that he was a man known to have a capacity for strong leadership, a reputation for independence, but perhaps most crucially a proven background of support for a view of European integration which preserved a strong role for the states.[33] Doubtless many were surprised when Giscard so quickly seized the opportunity to make his distinctive mark by expressing his immediate preference for the option of producing a single report from the Convention, not a series of options, a report which would take the form of a Constitutional Treaty. Moreover, Giscard has shown himself to be markedly undeterred by the complexity problem – namely that the choice for a Constitutional Treaty itself begged the question of 'fit' and coherence with what needs to be carried over from the old Treaties in terms of institutional provisions, legal bases, and policy frameworks, and what needs to be decided new from scratch. To that end, he instituted the group of legal experts from the European Union institutions, which has been charged with leading the way towards the drafting of Part Two of the Constitutional Treaty.[34] Indeed, one could surmise that the impact and effect of Giscard within the Convention and its work could be said to be one of the unintended and unexpected consequences of the process, rather than one of the checking factors serving the interests of member states, presumed at the outset to be unwilling to countenance too dramatic a shift from the *status quo*.

Giscard has shown himself to be simultaneously both controlling and flexible in relation to the process of compiling the Treaty. Control has stemmed above all from the insistence on issuing separate tranches of articles as these are approved by the Praesidium. This makes it more difficult for those Convention members who are not on the Praesidium and who therefore have little sense of the overall enterprise to address their comments to what they anticipate might be the final structure of the Constitutional Treaty. Furthermore, to the considerable disadvantage of national parliamentary members of the Convention who find it particularly difficult to fulfil their mandate to stay in touch with the views of their constituencies, very short deadlines have been given for submitting amendments and reactions to each fresh tranche of draft articles.

There is also evidence from plenary debates that Giscard has effectively controlled some of the most influential voices on the Convention – that is, those who are on the Praesidium and who are therefore privy to the early drafts of Treaty articles and to the Praesidium's own discussions about the direction the new Constitutional Treaty should take – by using some form of cabinet collective responsibility to muzzle those who have argued their case for a different view, but who have lost out, in the Praesidium's private meetings. Thus there is no question of Praesidium debates being replayed in public in the plenary and Praesidium members did not present formal amendments to the draft articles. The Commission, with its numerically small representation (both full members are also members of the Praesidium), is particularly affected by the adoption of this approach since only its alternate members, who are not politicians of stature but rather senior officials, are left unfettered by the application of such a doctrine of collective responsibility. This effectively turns around what might have been thought to be a *coup* for the Commission, namely to have both of its full members on the Praesidium, and turns it into a double-edged sword in terms of plenary debates and the capacity to propose amendments.

Furthermore, control has manifested itself in Giscard's own summaries of plenary debates at the conclusion of individual Convention sessions, in his presentations from time to time of the next steps which the Convention should take to advance its mandate, and in summaries of plenary meetings and Working Group meetings drawn up by the Secretariat (which doubtless receive political approval before they are published). These latter summaries have not always received unanimous support from 'embedded' Convention watchers as faithfully representing the debate. From time to time, they have seen a particular point receiving very strong support from individual Convention members, where the meeting summary represents this as merely involving 'a number of Convention members'. However, there is nothing surprising in this, as the role of the minute taker in a meeting has since time immemorial offered the opportunity to control the agenda as well as to present the outcomes of deliberations in a particular light.

As to flexibility, this has been demonstrated by the willingness to countenance the creation of new sub-groups of Convention members to deal with problems and issues as they have arisen, whether the Working Group on Social Europe which was set up right at the end of the Working Group phase in response to a bottom-up movement of Convention members, or the discussion circles on specific matters such as the Court of Justice, budgetary matters and latterly the question of taxation. It is also evident from Giscard's responsiveness to changing political contexts, such as his willingness to 'pull' the periodic report which he had hitherto delivered to each European Council meeting, when faced with the risk of being almost completely squeezed out of the agenda at the Spring 2003 European Council in the wake of the UN Security Council debacle and the launch of the US/UK military action in Iraq. At the same time, it became clear that this 'loss of face' was being immediately counterbalanced by close collaboration with the Greek Presidency to try, ultimately unsuccessfully, to implement a plan for the European Council to meet specifically to deal with Convention matters on 30 June 2003.

What was particularly clear throughout the whole process was that there remained a signal lack of clarity about what the final product would look like, both in terms of the final versions of draft provisions to which literally hundreds of amendments were proposed by Convention members and in terms of the overall shape of the Constitution, and the position of this 'product' upon which might be termed the continuum of views especially on institutional questions which connects the intergovernmentalists and federalists involved in the Convention. This has fuelled some conspiracy theorists who have suggested that the final proposed Constitutional Treaty will magically appear in large measure from Giscard's back pocket, or indeed from his top hat, in the manner of the magician's proverbial rabbit. Furthermore, some of those involved in the Convention regularly expressed displeasure at finding what they believed to be unwarranted departures in the articles issued by the Praesidium from what *they* perceived to be the 'results' of the Convention's work so far, embodied in its plenary discussions and its Working Group reports especially.[35] But so much has been said within the Convention, with so many different meanings and purposes, that gleaning a *single* consensus from these expressions of view is inevitably a judgemental exercise. To that extent, one person's consensus is another's dissensus, as the contested summaries of Convention meetings have made clear. For the purposes of the argument in this chapter what is most important is that lack of clarity about the overall output can lead to competing and contesting positions being advanced about the extent to which the final product will or will not be innovatory compared to the current state of European constitutional law. For example, Jean-Luc Dehaene, Vice-President of the Convention, called it 'evolution not revolution',[36] stressing that there will be much that is familiar to *cognoscenti* of the existing Treaties in whatever is eventually proposed by the Convention. Usefully, for observers of the Convention, the reports on the separate tranches of articles and key Working Group Reports which were produced in quick succession in Spring 2003 by the UK House of Lords Select Committee on the European Union[37] stressed in each case 'what was new' and 'what was old', and above all what was omitted in the new text from what was old, such as the reference to 'ever closer union amongst the peoples of Europe' which did not appear in the Praesidium's draft of Articles 1-16 of the draft Constitutional Treaty.[38]

It is this focus on the new/old combination of constitutional *acquis* refracted into the new Constitutional Treaty via the prism of the Convention's deliberations, and the creation of the sense of an autonomous Convention *acquis*, which leads from the focus on the Convention as process into a final reflection in this chapter upon questions of constitutional substance. This is the last step in this chapter's endeavour to provide a close description of how the Convention is simultaneously both rooted in the 'old' constitutional framework of the EU, as well as constantly toying with innovations and new ideas. This section will concentrate upon just a small number of substantive issues which have taxed the Convention, namely the treatment of fundamental rights in the Constitutional Treaty, the issues of sovereignty and supremacy in relations between EU law and national law and between the EU and the member states, and the questions of competence division and exercise.[39]

The substantive dimension of Convention-watching: working towards a European Constitution?

Rights; supremacy/sovereignty; competences. These are three key issues which will shape the final constitutional settlement suggested by the

Convention when it concludes its deliberations (and hands, of course, the torch of reform to the IGC). They are issues which go to the heart of the question: what is the European Union and what functions ought it to serve? I shall examine each in turn, the point being not to answer the questions which the Convention must face, but again to show how the Convention faces the delicate task of blending innovation and *acquis*, especially in so far as it cannot ignore the considerable extent to which the EU as it stands, at least as a proto-constitutional order, is a judicial creation. They also go to the heart of the fear that a formal constitutional settlement risks disturbing the delicate balance which underpins the current constitutional framework.[40]

It is hard to imagine a modern liberal polity with constitutional pretensions without some form of (binding) bill of rights as a definitive statement of social, political and civic values (as opposed to *ad hoc* protection of fundamental rights via the more elastic concept of general principles of law which is the *status quo* under EU law at present). How should the Constitutional Treaty take up this challenge? In that context, what should it do with the pre-existing but currently non-binding Charter of Fundamental Rights for the EU?

Given the United Kingdom's signal awkwardness in the context of the drafting of the Charter during the course of 2000, and its double insistence on both the inclusion of certain 'horizontal' clauses which would limit the scope and effect of the Charter if it were legally binding and the apparently unconditional rejection of the possibility of the Charter as drafted ever being adopted as a legally binding instrument, the position taken by the UK in the course of the deliberations of the Working Group on the legal status of the Charter was widely thought of as an important breakthrough.[41] While insisting again on the further strengthening of the horizontal clauses, the UK did not dissent from a 'consensus' view that the Charter ought to be incorporated as legally binding into the Constitutional Treaty, a view which was widely shared in plenary debates on this question. Far from settling all the relevant issues, however, the effect of this changed political determination on the part of a previously dissenting member state has been to open more questions than it has answered.[42]

A first line of enquiry concerns the nature of the invocation of the Charter as a legally binding part of the new constitutional framework which the Convention is working on. Should it be incorporated 'by reference', while remaining in a separate document indirectly given legal force? Or should it be incorporated as an integral and explicit part of the text of the Constitutional Treaty? If the latter solution is adopted, the next question must be: where in the Constitutional Treaty does it belong? At the beginning, before the general principles of the Union itself are articulated? In the middle of Part One of the Constitutional Treaty, which is destined to set out the constitutional framework of the Union? In a separate Part Two or Part Three of the Treaty, where its separateness will not break up the flow of the rest of the constitutional text? Or in an Annex or Protocol to the Constitutional Treaty, where it risks looking somehow downgraded in relation to the rest of the constitutional documentation? One factor may influence the location debate quite substantially. While the Charter was drafted on an 'as if' presumption, which reflected an intention to draft a text which was capable of being given legal force without further alteration, it was also drafted on the assumption it was a separate text to the Union treaties. Thus its final provisions or horizontal clauses not only contain the infamous attempts to ensure that the Charter could not be interpreted as extending the scope of Union competence and that its effects *vis-à-vis* the member states would be limited (see especially Article 51 of the Charter), but also provisions which protect the integrity of legal fundamental rights protection under national law, Union law and international law, for the benefit of individuals (see especially Article 53). Since the Convention appears resolved to incorporate the Charter as part of the Constitutional Treaty largely unamended, then it would perhaps do best to think about the questions which framed the intentions of those who drafted the Charter of Rights before deciding on the question of location.

Once the issue of location is settled, there remains the question of the relationship between the Charter and other sources of fundamental rights. The distinctive character of the Union's hitherto judge-led system of enforcement of fundamental rights, which has been based on Article 220 EC ('the Court shall ensure that the law is observed') and Article 6(2) TEU (which is effectively a codification of Court case law), has been its dynamic and fluid character. This included the possibility that the Court could refer to a substantial variety of possible sources of 'Community fundamental rights', including national constitutional traditions and different international law instruments, including but not confined to the European Convention on Human

Rights and Fundamental Freedoms ('ECHR'). To what extent should this *acquis* be carried forward into the post-Constitution era, or should the Charter become an *exclusive* source of the Union's fundamental rights, perhaps in combination with the ECHR alone? In its draft, the Praesidium suggested a combination of incorporating the Charter in an annex or protocol (Article 5(1)) and recognising that fundamental rights will continue as unwritten general principles of law (Article 5(3)). Oddly, though, it chose to refer in the latter provision only to the ECHR and the national constitutional traditions, failing to recognise that the Court of Justice has also frequently referred to other fundamental rights sources such as the International Covenant of Civil and Political Rights and the European Social Charter in its case law. In addition, the Praesidium's proposal also suggested a specific provision allowing accession – at a future date – by the Union to the ECHR, a proposal long supported by the influential House of Lords Select Committee on the European Union, amongst other voices.[43]

Finally, there is the sticky question of the content of the Charter and its relationship to the rest of EU law. There are substantial areas of overlap between the Charter and other provisions of EU law that will need to be included in the constitutional framework, whether in Part One on general principles and constitutional structure, or in Part Two on policies. Adjustment of the two sets of provisions to each other, or at least cross-reference, will be essential to ensure harmony of interpretation.[44] Article 52(2) of the Charter already recognises the overlap issue, by requiring that rights recognised by the Charter which are based on EU law are exercised in accordance with the conditions of the EU treaties. This seems to suggest that two sets of provisions could co-exist comfortably. However, what would be the outcome if the Convention were to decide – for reasons of constitutional aesthetics and in the interests above all of simplification – to eliminate overlap between the Constitutional Treaty itself and the Charter by ensuring that rights provisions appeared only once. Given the presumption that the Charter will stay unchanged – at least in relation to its substantive content – this would suggest that all rights issues within EU law are supposed to be settled primarily according to the precepts of the Charter, including its controversial horizontal clauses. This could shift the balance in relation to existing 'rights' cases under EU law as it stands, such as the right to non-discrimination on grounds of nationality, which exists under the EC Treaty *primarily* in order to curb national interferences with the evolution and functioning of the internal market, and associated flanking policies which contribute to socio-economic integration. This is a different *telos* to a fundamental rights Charter, and raises an important question about the dual functions of 'rights' under EU law as it stands. At this stage, the most plausible prediction which can be made is that whatever solution is chosen by the Convention and the IGC, there will be a substantial task for the Court of Justice to determine the scope and effects of rights provisions of both the Charter and the other sections of the new Constitutional Treaty, once the new settlement comes into force (assuming it does). Its task here will be to create synergies between the wider and already embedded *acquis* which it has developed in concordance with the existing treaties, and the *acquis* of the Convention and the new constitutional settlement.

The EU is a post-national polity, suspended between national polities and international regimes. The challenges of ensuring legitimate and effective governance will necessarily give rise to some difficult questions about how to articulate both the longstanding (judicial) principle of the supremacy of the law of the EU and the gradual consequential transformation of the traditionally singular sovereignty of Westphalian states into the shared sovereignty of a multi-level governance structure. How should each of these judicial principles be reflected in the Constitutional Treaty? For the UK, it was logical to object to the expression used in Article 1 of the Praesidium's first draft of the Treaty to the effect that 'this Constitution establishes the Union',[45] since the clear derivation from the international law nature of the Union is that the member states *establish the Union* and that the powers of the Union *flow from* the member states, so that the Constitution has only a derived and not an original status. The language of the Praesidium's draft subtly crosses the bridge between regime and polity, and challenges concepts of Westphalian sovereignty in the founding states. The explicit reference to the primacy of EU law in Article 9(1) of the Praesidium's draft also riled the UK. However, the statement that 'the Constitution, and law adopted by the Union Institutions in exercising competences conferred on it by the Constitution, shall have primacy over the law of the member states' is – as many commented in the plenary debate on 5 March 2003 – quite unexceptionable in view of the position under EU law as it stands. Take the Court's statement in 1964, in *Costa* v. *ENEL* that

'The transfer by the States from their domestic legal systems to the Community legal system of the rights and obligations arising under the Treaty carries with it a permanent limitation of their sovereign rights, against which a subsequent unilateral act incompatible with the concept of the Community cannot prevail.'[46]

Quite apart from what that statement asserts about the nature of what was then 'Community law', one of the most controversial statements concerned the so-called 'permanent' limitation of sovereign rights. We will return to this in a moment. Staying with the supremacy question, for the moment, it is still worth considering whether or not it is indeed quite unproblematic to insert a supremacy clause into the Constitutional Treaty, on the grounds of the fact that this is already a facet of the Union's constitutional order.[47] What the insertion could signal would be an important step towards the merging of the 'judicial constitution' and the formal legal constitution being worked on by the Convention. It could be said that this is in the spirit of Article 6(2) TEU, referred to above, which was introduced by the Treaty of Maastricht and codifies some aspects of the Court's case law on fundamental rights. Equally it is clear that this provision does not refer to the complex case law in which the Court has addressed the question of the extent to which member states are bound by the Union's fundamental rights guarantees when they are acting in some way in implementation of, or within the scope of, EU law. One thing is for sure, that case law does not speak with a single voice, and what is more, its interpretation is highly controversial amongst legal academics. Partly to preserve the integrity of EU law as a system, the Council Legal Service was heavily involved in seeking to bridge the gap between the Court's case law and the text of the Charter, including its restrictive horizontal clauses, through the drafting of the 'explanations' published alongside the Charter in October 2000.[48] These explanations referred to the Court's existing case law on the effects of the Union's fundamental rights *vis-à-vis* the member states as a *statement of the present law*. The lesson of this saga is, of course, that codification or consolidation[49] of the 'judicial constitution' is by no means unproblematic, and as Dougan makes clear this would be the case as well with supremacy.[50]

One area of debate would be the precise meaning of the supremacy principle, whether as general principle of hierarchy or as specific conflicts-resolution tool. That point is not insuperable, if one accepts that such a constitutional provision would in turn require substantial judicial elaboration over a period of time, and into that elaboration would be built in the different macro- and micro-level functions of the supremacy principle and associated legal doctrine, with the Court of Justice drawing upon the rich judicial *acquis* since *Van Gend en Loos* and *Costa* v. *ENEL* and perhaps adapting it to the changed circumstances generated by the Convention and the IGC. Furthermore, the argument that to include the supremacy principle is to draw attention to a facet of EU law best left hidden and visible only to legal experts and other elites is constitutionally disreputable. On the other hand, there are problems as it stands with the apparent generality of the principle set out in Article 9(1) if it does indeed purport to apply to the whole of the Union as a single legal edifice, including the old second and third pillars. Even if the Union becomes a single legal entity, the now 'subterranean pillars'[51] will continue to have legal and political effects, especially in terms of the differing types of competences given to the institutions and the varying effects of the instruments in relation to different areas of Union activity. A distinction will continue to be drawn between 'first pillar' matters, to which the principle of supremacy is currently limited, perhaps now joined by the third pillar, if the developing trend towards 'communitarisation' of all aspects of justice and home affairs policy continues, and the area of Common Foreign and Security Policy. A principle of supremacy drawn from the case law of the Court of Justice on the EC Treaty is simply inappropriate to this latter field of Union activity.

Above all, though, the inclusion of the supremacy principle – like the reference to the foundational nature of the Constitution in the Praesidium's draft of Article 1 – draws attention to the possibility that the Union is bridging the gap between regime and polity. The formal assertion of supremacy in this way heightens the tension between the EU legal order and the national legal orders by reinforcing the fact that in many respects, as things stand at present, the various systems make incommensurable claims, especially about so-called 'competence-competence' (the power to determine the legal scope of competence), and that serious conflicts are generally avoided by judicial interpretation of these incommensurable claims, not by the intractable pursuit of fundamentally incompatible principles such as the supremacy of EU law or the sovereignty of the member states under international law. To assert as much in the Constitutional Treaty may be to scratch at the evident sensibilities of many national constitutional courts, many of which prefer to rationalise the supremacy of EU law by reference to their own constitutional systems rather than the logic supplied by the Court of Justice, not to mention public opinion in a number of member states. Of course, that may be the intended effect, but there is no doubt that crossing that particular rubicon will still require something akin to a constitutional revolution in Europe and in the member states.

The reference to 'permanent limitation' in *Costa* v. *ENEL* seemed to some to suggest that a member state could not secede from the EC/EU – a point flatly contradicted in 1981 when Greenland seceded (as part of the untangling of its relations with Denmark). The way in which the old will blend with the new in interesting ways in the 'new' Union concerns the likely inclusion of a secession or voluntary withdrawal clause.[52] The first draft of the clause presented by the Praesidium seems to imply a slightly different emphasis to the position elaborated for Canada and the case of Quebec by the Canadian Supreme Court,[53] which introduced a clear duty on the part of all concerned to negotiate in good faith should a majority of the people of Quebec decide that they wished to secede from the Canadian federation. The proposed Article 46 of the Constitutional Treaty is premised on the 'decision to withdraw', which is a unilateral act taken in accordance with the constitutional requirements of each member state. Thereafter, the assumption is withdrawal will indeed occur, with the Union negotiating and concluding an agreement for withdrawal, and the seceding member state is excluded from the Council's discussions and decisions on the withdrawal agreement. The framework thus assumes an immediate reinstitution of the arm's length relationship between members and non-members. Interestingly, in contrast to Canada, where much important constitutional doctrine, such as on the twin principles of constitutionalism and democracy, has been judicially elaborated in the context of the whole issue of Quebec's potential secession and ongoing 'difference' from the rest of Canada, there have been no judicial interventions thus far on this issue.[54]

Turning, finally, to the issue of competences, it is widely thought – wrongly, quite probably – that there has been an unstoppable 'competence creep' in which the EU and its institutions have gradually encroached upon the (protected, sovereign) spheres of the member states.[55] Even if the argument is largely wrongheaded, and is based on a perverted view of the politics of law-making in the EU context as a politics of winners and losers,[56] how should the Convention react to the argument when it is certainly true that the system governing competence attribution, exercise and control is hardly a paragon of clarity in the EU and could certainly benefit from an overhaul? If the choice is for some sort of systematisation of types of competence and areas of competence, whatever the terminology used there will be little assistance from the Court's case law. Notwithstanding its usage of the terms exclusive and shared competence in the external relations sphere, the way in which the Court has approached the question has simply not been rationalised in this way. On the contrary, it *has* used the principle of attribution, which naturally the Praesidium's draft intends to preserve in Article 8(2), as the basis for establishing and testing the limits of competence by examining the scope and context of each individual legal basis to ensure that measures adopted on that basis correspond not only to the specific terms of that legal basis, but also to the wider *ethos* of EU law. That was the clear implication of the Court's rather contested judgement in the *Tobacco Advertising Directive Case*,[57] in which it declared in quite trenchant terms the outer limits of EU competence in respect of the regulation of cross-border advertising of tobacco products, both in relation to the regulation of the internal market and also in relation to the question of the protection of public health.

In terms of the existence of competence, attribution is all that can be found in the treaties as they are presently drafted, along with a vast number of legal bases, some of which are more carefully delineated than others, and of which Article 308 EC giving an implied power to regulate matters falling within the scope of the objectives of the Treaty is the most controversial. In addition, the Court has also evolved additional judicial principles such as the preemption of national legislative competence and the doctrine of implied powers to buttress the attribution principle from the point of view of the efficacy of EU governance. Other principles, such as subsidiarity and proportionality, govern only the *exercise* of competence. The important point to be made about draft provisions on categories of competence prepared by the Praesidium is not simply that they are inelegantly drafted. That is probably a resolvable difficulty. More serious is the fact that the attempt to introduce a 'categories' approach drawn from the experience of other (national) federations does not appear to fit well with the existing approach to competences which constitutes the *acquis communautaire* in this area. One can anticipate, therefore, that a move in this direction could precipitate considerable uncertainty as the institutions, and especially the Court, adjust to the new approach which is likely to be prescribed by the Convention and the IGC.

Conclusions

This chapter has offered a close examination of some key aspects of the emergent 'new' European Constitution, or draft Constitutional Treaty, via a focus on the process and substance which shape the work of the Convention on the Future of the Union. The chapter had a set of very modest objectives, namely to link debates about the Convention process to the substance of constitution-building and to show the influence of both the old Union *acquis* and the new mixed *acquis* of the Convention itself on the shaping of an anticipated new constitutional settlement for the EU. It is clear that in some cases the fit between the two is quite unsatisfactory, and this will generate legal and perhaps political uncertainty for a substantial period of time. Above all, in this context, simplification – that old mantra – can by no means be guaranteed. The Convention's work has undoubtedly provoked quite strong reactions, ranging from fierce optimism to rather depressed pessimism, even amongst those who share the view that constitutionalism can *and should*, if pursued effectively as a set of premises about legitimate rule, offer some sort of legitimacy surplus to the presently much maligned EU. Balance is clearly a key issue: balancing the interests of the various constituencies with a stake in the Convention to ensure maximum acceptability of its final product; balancing growing scepticism amongst publics about political institutions with the evident sense of goodwill towards European institutions frequently charted in Euro-barometer polls which indicates that Europe ought to be given a decent chance to establish itself; finally, and perhaps most crucially, balancing the new and the old in the Constitutional Treaty, and re-engaging with one of the oldest conundrums of legitimacy, namely balancing the responsiveness of institutions including guarantees of participation, with the need for effective governance and leadership in an ever more uncertain world.

Notes

[1] Duff, 2003.

[2] de Búrca, 1999.

[3] Most famously the German Federal Constitutional Court on the Treaty of Maastricht and the German constitution: *Brunner* [1994] 1 CMLR 57.

[4] Case 294/86 *Parti Ecologiste 'Les Verts'* v. *Parliament* [1986] ECR 1339. It repeated the point in Opinion 1/91 *Draft Agreement on a European Economic Area (EEA)* [1991] ECR I-6079. It is sometimes remarked upon that the Court has not repeated this point since the European Union famously ran aground on the sands of the legitimacy question, in the wake of the Maastricht ratification debacle.

[5] Some commentators caution that since the inception of the EU – i.e. the entry into force of the Treaty of Maastricht in 1993 – the Court of Justice has avoided 'constitutional' language, and has certainly not characterised the overall 'pillar framework' introduced by the Treaty on European Union as the EU's constitutional charter, as it did for the EC Treaty in *Les Verts*.

[6] de Witte, 2002.

[7] On the role of the *acquis communautaire* in relation to the governance of the EU see Wiener, 1998.

[8] E.g. Kohler-Koch, 1999; Church and Phinnemore, 2002: 15; Fischer, 2000.

[9] Shaw, 2003.

[10] Ophuls, 1966.

[11] Case 26/62 *Van Gend en Loos* v. *Nederlandse Administratie der Belastingen* [1963] ECR 1 at p12. See also Case 6/64 *Costa* v. *ENEL* [1964] ECR 585.

[12] *Van Gend en Loos*, p12; emphasis added.

[13] See generally on this Shaw, 2000a, Chapter 5.

[14] On the latter two points, see Vergés Bausili in this volume. See also Weatherill, 2003b.

[15] Bellamy and Castiglione, 2002. This has not extended, as noted above n.4, to the Court of Justice.

[16] Von Bogdandy, 2000.

[17] Weiler, 2002: 568.

[18] Giscard d'Estaing, 2002: 11.

[19] The involvement of a large number of Convention members concerned about precisely this question in terms of the acceptability of their own work in the initiative to persuade governments to hold a 'single' referendum on the European constitution in 2004 may have the capacity to change perceptions in this field, especially if it gains support amongst political elites at national level, and thus a coalition of national and European level elites is created. On the referendum initiative see CONV 658/03, 31 March 2003, Referendum on the European Constitution. This is an issue which is supported by eurosceptics and federalists alike, albeit for different reasons. Further information on these initiatives and ideas can be found on the website of the Initiative and Referendum Institute Europe (http://www.iri-europe.org/).

[20] Shaw, 2003.

[21] Closa, 2003.

[22] Attempts to capture more of this promise of deliberation are evident in mid-stream changes to how the Convention works introduced by the Praesidium, such as the

innovation of more frequent plenary meetings, the reduction in speaking time, and the decision to allow spontaneous interventions through the raising of 'blue cards', all designed to reduce the tendency of the plenary to be a sequence of 'soap-box' speeches: see 'Convention faces change of philosophy test', www.euobserver.com, 27 February 2003.

23 http://european-convention.eu.int/.

24 Those with a more casual or occasional interest should turn to websites such as the Federal Trust EU Constitution Project (www.fedtrust.co.uk/eu_constitution) which observe the Convention from the outside.

25 CONV 369/02 of 28 October 2002.

26 A term used by Convention Vice-Chairman Jean-Luc Dehaene, as quoted in Crum, 2003.

27 Objections have come notably from Convention members in political factions which are not represented in the Praesidium, such as the Green/EFA working collaboration on the Convention and the GUE/NGL group.

28 See CONV 250/02 Simplification of the Treaties and Drawing up of a Constitutional Treaty, 10 September 2002. It is unsurprising that the Secretariat has expertise on the specific question of simplification, because amongst its members is Hervé Bribosia, whose previous work included acting as Rapporteur on the European University Institute's much quoted pre-Nice project on simplification of the treaties, which was sponsored by the European Commission: Robert Schuman Centre, 2000. For commentary, see Feus, 2001.

29 See n.24 above.

30 CONV 528/03 of 6 February 2003 (Articles 1-16); CONV 571/03 of 26 February 2003 (Articles 24-33); CONV 602/03 of 14 March 2003 (Articles on finance); CONV 614/03 of 14 March 2003 (Articles on freedom, security and justice); CONV 647/03 of 2 April 2003 (Part Three: General and Final Provisions); CONV 648/03 of 2 April 2003 (Articles 43-46; Union membership); CONV 649/03 of 2 April 2003 (Article 42: Union and its immediate environment); CONV 650/03 of 2 April 2003 (Articles 33-37; democratic life of the Union).

31 CONV 369/02, n.24 above, Article 5.

32 CONV 528/03, n.29 above, Article 7.

33 See Hoffmann in this volume. See, for example, his advocacy of a cautious approach to enlargement, in the post-euro era: Giscard d'Estaing and Schmidt, 2000.

34 CONV 529/03 of 6 February 2003 Remit of the group of experts nominated by the Legal Services. The group has already produced one report and one addendum: CONV 618/03 of 17 March 2003; CONV 618/03 ADD 1 of 20 March 2003.

35 E.g. Hain, 2003; see also the interventions by Alain Lamassoure and others at the discussion of the Report of Working Group on Complementary Competences at the plenary of 7-8 November 2002

36 Dehaene, 2003: 6.

37 See the numerous reports available at http://www.parliament.the-stationery-office.co.uk/pa/ld/ldeucom.htm.

38 CONV 528/03, n.29 above. The term 'ever closer union' originated in the Preamble to the EEC Treaty, and was taken up in Article 1 of the Treaty on European Union.

39 See also on this Vergés Bausili, in this volume.

40 See the discussion of Joseph Weiler's position at n.16 above.

[41] Final Report of the Working Group, CONV 354/02, 22 October 2002.

[42] See generally de Búrca, 2003 and Brand, 2003.

[43] This was the view taken by the HL Select Committee in its report on the Charter: *EU Charter of Fundamental Rights*, 8th Report, 1999-2000, HL Paper 67. It repeats the view in a more recent report: *The Future Status of the EU Charter of Fundamental Rights*, 6th Report, 2002-2003, HL Paper 48.

[44] de Búrca, 2003: 29 *et seq*.

[45] CONV 528/03, n.29 above.

[46] Case 6/64 above n.10 at p594.

[47] See the cautionary comments in Dougan, 2003: 5-6.

[48] Note from the Praesidium, Draft Charter of Fundamental Rights of the European Union, *Text of the Explanations of the complete text of the Charter as set out in CHARTE 4487/00, CONVENT 50,* CHARTE 4473/00, CONVENT 49, 11 October 2000 (http://www.europarl.eu.int/charter/convent49_en.htm).

[49] Consolidation is the term used by the House of Lords Select Committee on the European Union in a report on Articles 1-16: *The Future of Europe: Constitutional Treaty – Draft Articles 1-16*, 9th Report, 2002-2003, HL Paper 61, p17.

[50] Dougan, 2003.

[51] The disappearance of the Maastricht pillars 'underground' is an expressive point made by Dr. Kalypso Nicolaïdis in a presentation to the Federal Trust/UACES Study Group on the Convention, 7 March 2003.

[52] Draft Article 46, included in CONV 648/03, above n.29.

[53] *Reference by the Governor in Council, pursuant to s 53 of the Supreme Court Act, concerning the secession of Quebec from Canada* [1998] 2 SCR 217.

[54] For argument about the potential applicability of this approach to constitutional flexibility in the EU, see Shaw, 2000b.

[55] See, in contrast, the much more sophistcated diagnosis of the 'problem' of the competence system offered in Section 1 of Vergés Bausili's chapter in this volume.

[56] See Weatherill, 2003b: 46.

[57] Case C-376/98 *Germany* v. *Council and Parliament* [2000] ECR I-8419.

The Convention on the Future of Europe Thoughts on the Convention-Model

Lars Hoffmann[1]

Introduction

The Convention on the Future of the Union held its inaugural session on 28 February 2002. This is the second convention the European Union has created, following the self-styled Convention which drafted the Charter of Fundamental Rights in 2000. However, it is the first dealing directly with institutional and constitutional issues that lie at the very core of the Union's power basis. The first heading in the Laeken Declaration,[2] establishing the Convention, reads 'Europe at a Crossroads'. In other words, the Convention has been created to decide how the EU is going to deal with the problems and challenges it is currently facing. The overall functioning of the Union has been widely criticised: the EU is not democratic enough and lacks transparency. The past Intergovernmental Conferences in Amsterdam and Nice have produced two new treaties but also a whole list of 'leftovers' – issues of great importance that could not be resolved. With the increasing complexity of the Union and the necessity to expand and/or limit its competences, the stakes today are higher than ever before and national delegations sitting at the negotiating table in Nice and Amsterdam had been unable to strike a deal acceptable to all participants. Therefore, it has become clear that before it can be decided which direction Europe is going to take at the 'crossroads', the EU first needs to reverse out of this dead end. Valéry Giscard d'Estaing, the Convention President, declared at the opening session of the Convention, 'We are a Convention, we are not an Intergovernmental Conference [...] we are not a parliament [we are] a group of men and women meeting for the sole purpose of preparing a joint proposal. [...] If it succeeds [...] it will light up the future of Europe.'[3] If the Convention is indeed able to 'light up the future', it is likely that in case of future crossroads, the 'Convention-model' could become the pathfinder that the last two Intergovernmental Conferences in Amsterdam and Nice failed to become.

This paper gives a short analysis for the reasons for convening this Convention on the Future of the Union. It argues that the current Convention on the Future of the Union might offer not only a way out of the current dead end – into which the Amsterdam and Nice negotiations have led – but also a possible new way to successfully deepen the integration process. It argues that it is an ideal forum as it combines legal, political and public players and might thus be able to become a permanent institution that complements the simple ICG-model.

The first part of the paper gives a broad overview explaining the problems that the IGC-model has been facing. It looks at the deadlocks the last IGC in Nice has produced and explains the reasons behind them. The second part explains what mandate the Convention has been given and analyses the 'safety features' that the Laeken Summit attached to the Convention to prevent it from overshooting the mark. The third part argues that the Convention will need to secure broad support from its own members and civil society in order to put enough pressure on the forthcoming IGC to adopt its proposal. The final part argues that the Convention-model provides an ideal forum for institutional reform. It is a new body that is much more open and representative than any Intergovernmental Conference. The 'Convention-model' could become a constant feature in the European constitutional process replacing the simple ICG-model.

The limitations of the IGC-model

The process of European integration has witnessed four new treaties over the past two decades. The revision of existing treaties and the subsequent drafting of an additional one has been carried out by Intergovernmental Conferences (IGCs). The general feature of IGCs is that they act as both the guardians of existing European achievements and treaties – the *acquis communautaire* – and the ultimate sources of their revision.[4] Whereas the bulk of the IGC work is carried out by national ministers and government representatives, the most controversial and contested issues are left to the final summit of Heads of Government/State:

> Three types of issue were identified: a) those that could be kept out of the final discussions and for which agreement could be obtained before the European Council in Nice (Court of Justice and Court of First Instance, composition of Institutions other than the Commission); b) pivotal issues (qualified majority, reinforced co-operation) for which the Group of Representatives had a mandate to go as far as it could in order to arrive at significant agreements before Nice; and c) questions relating to the balance of power (weighting of votes, composition of the Commission), where there would be only a technical examination of the options on the table and the final decision would be left to the Heads of State or Government in Nice.[5]

However, in view of the results achieved in Amsterdam and Nice, the IGC-model seemed to lose its effectiveness mainly due to four different issues:

First, the issues that the last (and the forthcoming) IGCs were dealing with are more likely to lead to deadlock in negotiations. The stakes are rising as the possible solutions are much more likely to give national governments the impression that they are losing political influence within the Union's framework. Compromises are thus more unlikely because it is becoming more difficult to guarantee that negotiation outcomes result in win-win situations for all participants. Not only the last IGC in 2000, but also the one before that in 1996 reached deadlock, producing so-called 'leftovers' because governments were not able to compromise on certain 'taboo areas.'[6] In fact, the 2000 IGC in Nice was supposed to deal with the Amsterdam leftovers, i.e. issues the final summit of Heads of Government/State could not agree on in 1996 and thus had been left to be solved by the next IGC,[7] but it failed to do so in a satisfactory manner. If we take a closer look at these leftovers, it is clear that they are concerned with the very core of the Union's power structure. They are of huge political and economic importance and therefore have a great constitutional significance for the future outlook of the Union, in particular three issues: the composition of the Commission, the decision-making procedure in the Council (including the weighing of the votes) and the expansion of qualified majority voting into areas such as social policy and taxation.[8] As the leftovers Nice had to deal with were constitutional issues, the stakes were rising and member states became eager to make sure that their national position and influence within the power-structure of the Union would not be undermined. The EU found itself in a difficult situation: on the one hand it had important institutional and political issues to decide; on the other, because these issues were so important, it was unable to agree on a common denominator.

Second, there was the increasingly inflexible positions which member state governments insisted upon taking. It is important to note that 'in an IGC, each player carries a good deal of psychological baggage with him/her: perceptions are already skewed towards other players in expected ways which are generally known to all. The ability to surprise and gain tactical advantages is accordingly relatively limited and fraught.'[9] This baggage was accumulated over the last two IGCs in two ways. First, the list of issues that remained unsolved has become longer and second, the position of member states' governments has become more inflexible. This is a reinforcing process as after Amsterdam the different positions of the member states governments were openly analysed. Therefore, for a government to compromise on these positions would have meant to give in to the pressures exercised by others. Thus, the longer the negotiations went on and the more member state governments publicised their official positions the more unlikely it became that a compromise could be found. Additionally, governments were concerned with the need to return home claiming to have achieved a result which was particularly beneficial to their respective country. Although the IGC's closed-door mentality meant that the public was not fully aware of the extensive negotiations and horse-trading that went on in private, in Amsterdam and Nice there were simply not enough horses left to achieve a compromise that made everyone a winner. Deadlock was inevitable.

Third, the division between the member states increased. Even traditional alliances, foremost the Franco-German axis, were no longer working as effectively as they used to.[10] Due to the rising stakes neither the German nor the French government (who held the Presidency of Council) was willing to make a compromise that threatened their influence in Europe. The Franco-German 'slow-down' meant that the most effective partnership, on which European integration had relied and depended on since the Union was founded, was no longer able to lead the way out of the complicated negotiation process that unfolded in Nice.[11] The range of issues the Heads of Government/State could not agree on remained the same. Alliances hardly changed as larger and smaller countries were facing each other with respect to the reallocation of votes in the Council, the modification of the decision-making procedures (double or triple majority in the Council) and the future composition of the Commission. Moreover, poor and rich countries were arguing about policies (structural funds) and agricultural countries were opposing any enlargement of QMV in the area of the common agricultural policy (CAP). The negotiations soon reached a deadlock and the compromises made in the last minutes were far from satisfactory.[12]

Finally, the influence of European institutions was kept at a minimum. The Commission was denied a role as an official mediator, which is left entirely to the host country, which holds the Council Presidency. This is an important issue to consider because the Commission, as well as the European Parliament, would be in an ideal situation to play the role of a mediator as they are independent from the 'national taboo areas'. Although the Commission has been able to play a considerable role, especially under the Presidency of Jacques Delors, when it comes to the crucial issues and late night bargaining, even the Commission is reduced to a simple spectator. Normally, 'the Commission's influence would consist of three main sources: its near-monopoly on the technical expertise of the nature of treaty reform, a gate-keeper position *vis-à-vis* non-governmental interests, and close co-operation with both Council Secretariat and Presidency in the preparation of versions of Draft Treaty'.[13] This means that the Commission plays a mainly administrative and technical role. It is, however, not involved in the actual negotiations about factual treaty changes. It is left out of political decisions and can only try to exert influence by proposing its own suggestions and solutions. These, however, have no official status within the intergovernmental negotiations.

Compared to the Commission, that at least plays a role in the preparatory phase of IGCs, the role of the European Parliament has been even more minor. The EP only held an observatory position. There have been informative meetings between IGC delegations and the President of the Parliament, but the EP's impact on actual negotiations has been minimal.[14] Although it produces papers and opinions they are not given the same attention than proposals originating from the Commission. During the 2000 IGC, the EP President, Nicole Fontaine, was able to meet with representatives of the ministerial sessions that prepared the Nice Summit. Admittedly that was an improvement in the EP's position, but, prior to the Conference meeting of Heads of Government/State there was again only an informal meeting and exchanges of positions. During the 2000 IGC negotiations the Parliament was able to send two observers to the Group of Representatives. Which meant that they had no right to vote or exercise official influence. Although this was a major improvement of the EP's status compared to previous IGCs it still proves that the European Parliament has not been able to become an equal and fully recognised participant within the IGC process. In the following it will be argued that giving the EP an official status in the IGC is a possibility to increase legitimacy and the Convention could be the ideal framework to do exactly that.

So, EU institutions were formally part of the process, yet not able to exercise any official powers. The IGCs, due to their purely intergovernmental approach to treaty reform, denied the European institutions the role of an independent mediator, necessary to bring the different interests of the member states' governments within the reach of an efficient compromise: 'Whereas the initial agenda of the IGC may be influenced by EU institutions (notably the Commission and the European Parliament), the outcome is a mediated negotiated compromise, supported by a consensus of the member states'.[15]

Intergovernmental Conferences have proved to be a vital part of the European Union's integration process. Especially the negotiations concerning the European Monetary Union, which were successful due to the Franco-German leadership and in 1991 the active support of Commission President Delors. However, as an intergovernmental institution, the conference has encountered great difficulties during the last two IGCs in dealing with issues that relate to the constitutional order of the Union which potentially imply shifts in the Union's power structure. The inflexibility of the participants makes the task of finding a compromise more difficult as the different delegations can only act within their specific 'area of acceptability' and have certain 'boundaries' they can not cross (e.g. QMV for taxation was completely taboo for the British government).[16] The will to embrace new approaches and the desire to make compromises in all areas of concern is very low. Therefore, the IGC-model, it seems, has come to a dead-end as far as 'big politics' are concerned. The integration process is currently deadlocked which is, in turn, aggravated by the looming enlargement, which demands substantial institutional and political changes. The Convention's President, Valéry Giscard d'Estaing made an excellent point in his Discours when he described the IGC (and the problems which are connected with it) as: '[...] an arena for diplomatic negotiations between member states in which each party sought legitimately to maximise its gains without regard for the overall picture.'[17]

The Convention's Framework

For the purposes of this paper it is important to understand the general framework within which the Convention is working. First, the Laeken Declaration made sure that the Convention consists of representatives from a wide range of institutions and the possible number of alliances is very large; and they vary according to the subject matter. As a British Labour MEP, you could be joining forces with the EP-delegation, with the parliamentary delegation (including representatives from national parliaments), the social democratic delegation or with the other British representatives. There are many more ways of liaising and forming alliances than in an IGC, where only representatives from (currently) fifteen national governments join the negotiations. In an IGC group, government representatives might join forces with other nationals but individual representatives will not 'belong' to different camps of interest. The decision concerning the kind of outcome the Convention will arrive at depends on what kind of alliances will be formed, which guiding force will be the strongest and how much of a compromise the different players are willing to make in order to achieve a consensus.

Second, the Convention was given a relatively broad and open mandate: 'in order to pave the way for the next Intergovernmental

Conference as broadly and openly as possible, the European Council has decided to convene a Convention composed of the main parties involved in the debate on the future of the Union. In the light of the foregoing, it will be the task of that Convention to consider the key issues arising for the Union's future development and try to identify the various possible responses.'[18] The IGC-model, as exercised in 1996 and 2000, is no longer able to provide efficient and effective solutions to the constitutional challenges currently facing the Union. In response, the Heads of Government/State decided at the Nice Summit to call for another IGC in 2004 and it requested the 2001 Laeken Summit to introduce a convention which would take over the preparatory work for that next IGC.[19] The Laeken Summit produced a declaration[20] which called for a Convention to be formed dealing with the issues the Union has to solve if it wants to work in a more efficient and democratic manner. The Declaration states that 'they [the European citizens] want the European institutions to be less unwieldy and rigid and, above all, more efficient and open.'[21] It is mainly an accumulation of questions which require answers if the Union is to be able to function properly and to have a democratic and legitimate structure. The questions were straight forward, open and broad and did not indicate any political preferences. Nevertheless, the Heads of Government/State at Laeken were, of course, careful enough not to set loose an uncontrollable body which might come forward with proposals too far from the *status quo*. As soon as the Convention got under way, national governments and Heads of Government/State begun to come forward with certain 'ideas' or 'suggestions' produced by their offices or even co-produced with other national leaders. The Franco-British initiative regarding the Presidency of the Council is one example.[22] The Heads of Government/State are making sure that they do not loose control over the Convention and they are also trying to encourage its members into taking viewpoints rather closer to their own.

Third, to make sure that the Convention's work does not drift from its original purpose, the Laeken Council has attached several 'safety features': its leadership was selected carefully by the Laeken Summit.[23] Valéry Giscard d'Estaing is an elderly statesman with an ingrained intergovernmental approach to the Union who is known for his 'personal' approach to politics meaning that he is neither likely to lose grip of the way the Convention is running nor of the actual drafting process of the future constitution. It is worth highlighting that the difference between the President of the first Convention on Fundamental Rights, Roman Herzog, and the President of the current Convention on the Future of the Union, Giscard d'Estaing, could not be more dramatic. Both have been presidents in their respective countries, but whereas Giscard d'Estaing has been a full-time politician, at a regional and national level in a unitary state, Roman Herzog is a lawyer and a former constitutional judge in a federal state. It is no coincidence that the federal judge is not heading the Convention that proposes a future constitutional framework for the Union. Considering his age and expertise, he is expected to have certain ideas about how the European Union should look like and is unlikely to change his mind on issues that he has been concerned with for over 40 years. Although Giscard d'Estaing is committed to the cause of the Union, he is not likely to turn it into a 'Superstate' with a clear cut federal constitution. His Presidency is therefore predictable and unlikely to slip out of his hands or those of the European Council. It seems the Council has calculated correctly. Giscard d'Estaing, so far, has initially kept himself in the background by organising a 'listening phase' aimed at initiating an exchange of views and setting into motion the internal dynamics which have taken over the Convention by the time the 'drafting phase' started at the beginning of 2003. Giscard has carefully orchestrated the work of the Convention and he has kept the strings in his hand resulting in the drafting phase being very much controlled by him as well as the Secretariat and the Convention Praesidium. The proposals and statements from him and his Secretariat do not suggest a strategy that would be too radical for the European Council.[24] Neither the first 'skeleton' draft treaty[25] nor the first 16 articles[26] presented in November 2002 and February 2003 respectively, have stirred up too much controversy, not even in the UK. He is therefore carefully stirring the Convention work towards a broadly supported consensus, which can then be used as a basis to mount pressure on the forthcoming IGC to adopt the Convention's constitutional proposal.

The limitation of time attached to the mandate is another safety feature to prevent the Convention producing a document at odds with the general ideas of the European Council. A period of 12 months is a very short period of time to produce a document that potentially gives answers to all the questions posed by the Laeken Declaration, bearing in mind that this document should also be able to serve as Europe's first constitution.[27] Yet, in this respect the Convention has already shown that it is developing its own dynamic for it has enlarged its own timeframe and the final outcome is now scheduled for the Thessaloniki Summit in June 2003 (as opposed to the initial finishing date of March 2003). In this context one must not forget that apart from the President and his two substitutes, all other Convention members have 'other jobs' to do. This means that their concentration will not be entirely devoted to the convention, instead it will be split between their work in Brussels and back home. Only the participating MEPs (up to a certain point at least) are also in a situation where they are able to concentrate their full attention onto the Convention, which gives them a distinct advantage over the other members.

It is no surprise, therefore, that the MEPs in the Convention form a very pro-active and relatively cohesive group within it. They have the distinct advantage of already being established in an internal network and knowing their way around Brussels (from an intellectual as well as logistical point), something the other Convention members (especially national MPs) first had to get used to. As the MEPs traditionally hold a more 'supranational' viewpoint with regards to the future of the Union than the Council, the Heads of Government/ State may have underestimated its potential impact on the final document. There are 16 MEPs taking part in the Convention and they have a considerable advantage over other delegations. They are based in Brussels, they have their internal and external networks and resources based there and they are used to working as a collective – usually together with the Commission and against the Council. Their position is by definition much more powerful due to institution as well as infrastructure reasons. National parliamentarians or government representatives might not ever have been to Brussels and find it difficult to join forces with other parliamentarians they have never met before. The EP Delegation is a coherent group used to working together. Also, the European Parliament, as argued above, has thus far been left out of the IGCs and so has had little impact on the constitutional changes of the Union in the past decades. This is not due to lack of interest but due to the fact that the Council did not allow any other institution to form part of the 'treaty-reform-team'. The MEPs, with their primary interest being by definition the workings of the EU, are highly motivated to take a very active part in this future-shaping Convention. This is the job they have been waiting for ever since the first EP elections back in 1979. Moreover, the internal divisions within the EP delegation are minimal and their common vision of a future EU much more defined than, for example, among national MPs or government representatives.[28] Moreover, MEPs will be able to devote a more substantial amount of time and thought to the Convention than their national counterparts and the government representatives. Observing the first months of the Convention, it is clear that it is the EP delegation who have exercised most pressure on Giscard to come forward with his ideas and set a clear agenda.[29]

A fourth characteristic of the framework of the Convention is the fact that it meets in public. As the Convention is composed of representatives from a wide range of different institutions and interests and it meets in public and is scrutinised by civil society, academia and the press, the kind of 'horse-trading-based negotiations' – typical for an IGC – are not possible. Not only are there many more players involved in the Convention than there ever were in the IGC – not necessarily in terms of numbers but in terms of the different institutions they represent – but also, the Convention meets in public and publicises its documents and papers, opening up the Convention to the European citizens and making itself as an institution considerably more transparent and representative. As it represents so many institutions and its members are scrutinised back in their home countries[30] it is much closer to the European citizens than an Intergovernmental Conference. Furthermore, the Laeken Declaration itself emphasised that a Forum should be established which gives civil society the opportunity to contribute to the discussion on the Future of Europe. 'In order for the debate to be broadly based and involve all citizens, a Forum will be opened for organisations representing civil society [...]. Their contributions will serve as input into the debate.'[31]

The Convention will have to deal with legal and political issues and its composition and links to the citizens puts it in an extraordinary position to do that. Under these conditions the Convention is much more likely to produce a legitimate document which will receive widespread support across Europe than either of the IGCs in Amsterdam and Nice were able to. The IGC-model, due to the lack of individual accountability, openness and transparency in the negotiation process, suffers from the same democratic deficit that characterises much of the Union's institutional order. The next IGC will have to consider the Convention's findings and proposals, and it will remain up to the

IGC to decide which parts – if any at all – it will accept and implement in a possible new treaty or even a constitution. The Laeken Council has attached several 'safety features' to the Convention, however, the findings of the Convention will have a big legitimacy-advantage and possibly the support of a considerable part of civil society as well as representatives of the EP, national parliaments, the Commission and even national governments (of the member states and all accession states). Under these conditions it may prove more difficult for the Heads of Government/State to turn down the outcomes of the Convention than to accept them.

How can the Convention be successful?

The Convention has been asked to produce a document, treaty or constitution, that not only copes with the constitutional questions arising from the enlargement process but that also paves the way for a new institutional structure that is closer to the citizens and is built on a more democratic and legitimate foundation. Every government participating in the next IGC will have a veto and can thus prevent the Convention's proposals from being implemented. Yet, it is crucial to note that striking down the suggestions and solutions provided by the Convention without providing an acceptable alternative – acceptable to all national government representatives and the Heads of Government/State – will be almost impossible for any government. It should be remembered that the very existence of the Convention is due to the fact that the previous Intergovernmental Conferences were not able to produce such a compromise. Nevertheless, to produce a document that will be successfully implemented as the first European constitution, the Convention will have to fully satisfy three different interest groups. Its own members, the forthcoming IGC, and the European citizens. The question therefore is, how can the Convention ensure that its constitutional treaty will be based on a consensus comprising the large majority of all three of these players?

First, the final document to be produced by the Convention will have the potential to serve as the first European constitution; it therefore has considerable symbolic weight. The chance to produce the first European constitution, and hence to secure a chapter in the history books, will provide the Convention with significant motivation to produce a coherent document.

To produce a document that is supported by a broad consensus will be extremely difficult as there are, due to its composition, a large number of different interests and ambitions dominant among the Convention members. Also, the alliances between the different members are not stable but vary according to the issue concerned. Of course there are some more important members in the Convention which have a greater importance and can exercise a greater impact than others. The President – supported by his Secretariat – is clearly the head figure who is dominating the Praesidium and can be expected to have an outstanding role in the drafting process. In addition there are the government representatives who are significant players and Giscard will be careful to draft a constitutional treaty which is endorsed by preferably all of them. The fact that many governments have replaced their representatives and sent Foreign Ministers into the Convention[32] shows that the governments are taking the Convention much more serious and are anxious to prevent it from agreeing on a constitutional treaty which they might find difficult to unravel during the following IGC. In addition to the government representatives, the MEPs have played an important role in the Convention. They had the distinct advantage of having an in-depth knowledge of the 'Brussels-world' and apart from anything else they have their offices and all the related logistics based there. Contrarily, national MPs were new to the Brussels scene and could not fall back on the same administrative infrastructure as the MEPs.

Therefore, Giscard knows that the only winning formula is to produce a constitutional treaty that has the potential to secure the broad support of both MEPs and government representatives. The impact of a document that receives something close to unanimous support among the Convention members is clearly much greater than that of a document that secures only the support of a simple majority. The Laeken Declaration makes it clear that the final document 'may comprise different options, indicating the degree of support which they received.[33] For the Convention to succeed – i.e. to produce a treaty which will not be (at least not significantly) changed by the forthcoming IGC – means that it will have to avoid producing an 'option paper' comprising different options for each treaty article. The document needs to be coherent and politically balanced so that it does not scare off, for example, the Danish or British Convention members, nor be too cautious to miss out on the support of, for example, the

German and Belgian ones. The problem may be that MEPs tend to be more ambitious and would prefer a more integrationist, even federal version, whereas government representatives are potentially more committed to a more intergovernmental solution. Therefore, it will be left to Giscard and the Secretariat to mediate between different influential forces in the Convention and to make sure that the final document is on the whole acceptable to most if not all of them. It should be noted that the possibility of drafting Europe's first constitution may function as a 'carrot' providing the much needed incentive to agree on a compromise acceptable to them and the Convention at large.

Second, the Convention will have to integrate the ideas and suggestions brought forward by civil society via the Forum. This might prove to be an excellent source of fresh input, especially since this sort of official link between the EU and civil society has never existed before. Although the designs and concepts provided by the Forum participants might not always be identical with the opinion of the majority of the Convention members, establishing a close co-operation and incorporating some of them into the final document would add to the credibility and legitimacy of the Convention and its output. It is therefore crucial that the Convention is able to incorporate some of the thoughts and ideas provided via the Forum, although it might add to the already difficult situation of finding a common denominator among the Convention's diverse membership. Yet, if the Forum approves the final outcome of the Convention's work, the latter will have achieved something the Union has failed to do so far – to get involved with its citizens in the integration process and bring the Union closer to them.

Moreover, the support of the Forum and the wider European public might also depend on whether the Convention will be able to make sure that its final document is more accessible than the current – highly complicated – treaties. The issue of language is central in bringing the Union closer to its citizens. People interact are more likely to be supportive of the EU if they understand exactly what it is about, where its competences lie and how its institutions function. Therefore, it might prove to be a successful approach if the new document were divided into two parts. The first one would contain the principle structures of the Union, referring to the composition and competences of its institutions and their interconnection. The second part would deal with the detailed decision-making procedures and explications of policies.[34] This idea would make the document much more accessible for European citizens and so might trigger greater interests and support from the public, the press and so put considerable pressure on the Heads of Government/State to adopt it at the next IGC.

Third, the Convention is only supposed to carry out the preparation work for the forthcoming IGC and without the member states' governments' unanimous support for the Convention's proposal, all efforts will have been in vain. The Convention's main task, which will dominate the final drafting of the Convention's proposals, is to satisfy the Intergovernmental Conference by presenting a document that gives clear answers to the questions asked in the Laeken Declaration. In fact, the arrival of Foreign Ministers in the Convention might make this task easier because it is unlikely that (during the IGC) they will be able to go back on issues they agreed upon during the Convention. Still, on the one hand, the Convention could present a rather uncontroversial document, which is consensus based and does not even upset the most eurosceptic governments. On the other hand, the Convention could put pressure on the IGC to guarantee its support. It could present a more integrationist treaty and simultaneously try to manoeuvre the Heads of Government/State into a situation where they cannot refuse the Convention's suggestions due to the large support that it receives throughout its own members, civil society and the press.

The Convention is set to go for the second option. The final document will not be an easy pill to swallow for the Intergovernmental Conference but it will have secured the overall support of the government representatives and will therefore be *de facto* acceptable. As argued above, presenting a coherent document not containing any alternative suggestions (from which the IGC could potentially pick and choose its favourite versions) will be of the highest priority. Also, co-operating closely with the Forum will increase the pressure on the IGC as it potentially adds legitimacy to the Convention's final document.

In addition, the Convention members and foremost its President, Valéry Giscard d'Estaing, will be motivated to see the Convention's outcome being implemented. He would become the 'Father of the

European Constitution' – a prospect which is likely to make sure that he will lobby the Heads of Government/State hard and to put public pressure on them to accept the Convention's final document. Of course, other Convention members will try the same but the lobbying power of Giscard d'Estaing will be very significant as he is the one the Heads of Government/State initially chose to preside over the Convention. Given that he was offered the task of chairing the Convention how could the IGC refuse its outcome if it is strongly supported by the man they put in place to supervise the process?

Therefore, if the Convention strikes the right balance, between producing a consensus based document that receives widespread public support, and is able to successfully lobby the next IGC, its output stands an excellent chance of becoming the first European Constitution. Despite the potential difficulties to secure sufficient support it can be expected that the Convention will produce a document that eventually will be accepted and implemented by the forthcoming Intergovernmental Conference. Not all Convention members will feel they have achieved a solution which matches their high ambitions; but it will be far more successful and effective than the failed attempts from the 1996 and 2000 IGCs.

Can the Convention-model complement the IGC-model?

With the difficulties the IGC-model has suffered in Amsterdam and Nice and with the potential success of the Convention looming, it has to be considered whether the Convention-model could amend the IGC-model on a permanent basis – leading to a potential amendment of Article 48 TEU.

The only argument against the institutionalisation of the Convention-model is that it would add a new layer to the already complicated institutional 'Legoland' of the Union of today. Already it is difficult to understand the decision-making process and the competences and interconnections between the European Parliament, the Commission and the Council, nevermind the working procedure of an Intergovernmental Conference. To add to all this a Convention which will be created only on an *ad hoc* basis will make things even more complicated and incomprehensive for the wider public. The composition of its members is seemingly based on a mathematical equation that is difficult to decode. The members of the Convention represent 32 different institutions: representatives from 15 different national governments, 15 different national parliaments (not considering the fact that, for example, Germany sends parliamentarians from two different Chambers), the Commission and the European Parliament. And this is not even counting the members representing parliaments and governments from the accession countries. Therefore, it may be questionable whether adding this new body to the institutional structure of the European Union will be counterproductive or not.

Considering the difficulties and problems the IGC-model has been faced with, particularly in Nice, the Convention has the potential to overcome these and be the preparatory instrument for future Intergovernmental Conferences. Referring back to the difficulties IGCs are potentially facing, it can be argued, that amending the IGC-model with the Convention, these difficulties may be overcome. It is true that the significance of issues will not be reduced because they are handled by a Convention. However, Convention members do not represent national governments in the same way that IGC participants do. Therefore the stakes are less high for the actual participants. They are less under pressure from official government lines than representatives negotiating in IGCs and they are more likely to present their own personal opinion and thus are able to take some pressure off high-stake issues. The Convention is not a clearly shaped arena with strictly arranged groups and alliances like it is so often the case during IGCs. This allows Convention members to take a much more flexible approach to the negotiations. They are taking part to find an effective and efficient solution acceptable to the large majority of participants. They are not there to push through 'issues of national principle' to improve the position of individual national governments in the European Union.

The issue of alliance is really a non-issue at the Convention. As argued before the number of possible alliances is much higher and therefore it is likely that several leading alliances will emerge. These alliances are much more open and flexible than those to be found in IGCs. Convention members can be – and often are – part of several groups. This also is likely to facilitate the negotiations and will help to produce satisfactory results. In addition, the influence of the European institutions could be greatly enhanced if the IGC-model was amended by the Convention-model. Both the Commission and the European Parliament have sent representatives to the Convention; the Committee of the Regions, the Economic and Social Committee, the European Social Partners and the European Ombudsman have all sent observers. The influence the European institutions are able to take in the Convention is likely to further benefit the outcome and to ensure that the Convention presents the next IGC with an effective and efficient proposal.

The problems the IGC-model has been facing will not disappear by amending Article 48 TEU and introducing a Convention before every IGC but it will facilitate the IGC's work, for it provides it with proposals that have received the approval of an extremely broad range of different representatives from throughout the Union. Member state governments will be able to settle critical issues – despite high stakes – thanks to the legitimacy advantage of the Convention. Its outcome cannot be regarded as biased to any (group of) member state(s) nor to the EU institutions due to its diverse composition, which has been agreed upon by the participants of the IGC themselves. As Paul Magnette points out: '[…] the governments agreed because, since the process was highly unforeseeable, they could all think that they would be able to maximise their interests – and otherwise they would still have the opportunity to minimise their costs during the following IGC.'[35]

Furthermore, in many respects the Convention can be considered to be an ideal mix of politics, law and citizen participation, which might be the key to future constitutional changes in an EU with a political, economic, and possibly even military framework. First, the Convention is a highly transparent and open institution. The admittedly complex composition of the Convention can also be regarded as one of its greatest strengths. It means that there is a much improved linear connection between the citizens and an official EU body. Consisting of MEPs, national parliamentarians and national government representatives the Convention is much closer to the citizens than an IGC. This is helped by the fact that the Convention holds its meetings in public and makes its working papers and documents freely available. Transparency and accountability – issues the Convention is supposed to reinforce in the Union – have a prime position in the Convention's working attitude. Already, we see members of the Convention travelling through Europe and taking part in conferences and public debates, or publishing their opinions and thoughts in national newspapers.[36] Convention members are actively trying to establish a link with citizens which can only be welcomed and which has been absent from the IGC-model.

Second, the Convention members are representative and can work very efficiently for they do not carry 'baggage' from previous negotiations. The vast majority of the members of the Convention are democratically elected as they are mostly members of national governments or parliaments,[37] while most participants of an IGC, apart from the national Ministers and the Heads of Government/State meeting at the final summit, are not directly democratically legitimised. They are mostly officials for which the ministers are ultimately responsible. A considerable part of the Convention's work is also done by unaccountable officials, most prominently the Secretariat with its head, John Kerr.[38] However, due to the Convention's inherently transparent character and the fact that submitted documents are made public in the name of the Convention's members, the level of accountability is undoubtedly higher in the Convention than in an IGC.

Convention members hold their position only temporarily, which has the great advantage that they do not have to perform in a way that ensures their re-election or re-nomination. They can thus concentrate fully on finding the most effective solution. That stands in sharp contrast to the work of an Intergovernmental Conference where Heads of Government/State are grilled back home about their achievements during the IGC. Their personal performance will be measured by whether they have been able to 'win a deal' that benefits their country; and this is likely to have considerable impact on their popularity back home. Thus, the Convention-model combines accountability and transparency with the advantage of being relatively independent from political implications 'back home' which makes it potentially more open-minded and flexible and will hence facilitate finding an effective compromise.

Third, it should not be forgotten that the IGC would lose neither its competences nor its importance. The findings of the current Convention will have to be presented to the forthcoming IGC and it is up to the latter to decide whether or not it will accept the findings, or at least in part. This arrangement is unlikely to change. The member states' governments will make sure that they always have the final say (including a veto option) about the proposals coming out of any future convention. Therefore, the 'IGC-model' of 'big politics' will not be challenged or replaced but rather enriched by a new component which looks like it is able to fix the flaws that the current system has stumbled over during the last two IGCs. Of course the Convention may seek to persuade the member states' governments to introduce a changed treaty amendment system whereby the IGC would be completely replaced by a simple Convention-model. However, no institution is likely to transfer its powers and competences and transfer them to a different body. That will be also true for the IGC. It will not allow the Convention-model to completely replace the IGC in its function as principal treaty amendment body, yet a change in Article 48 TEU might be appropriate to grant the Convention-model a permanent place alongside it.

Conclusion

Although IGCs have proved to be a remarkably successful forum for deepening the integration process and to give all member state governments the opportunity to participate equally in negotiations, it seems as if the current constitutional issues and questions cannot be tackled in this way as 'institutional reform divided and continues to divide the member states.'[39] The Convention is a new attempt to make the Union and its integration process more open and accountable. It seems to be more capable to solve the institutional and constitutional issues that the Union is currently facing than the IGC-model was in 1996 and 2000. Influential figures of the European Parliament delegation and the government representatives have emerged as the driving forces with the President trying to mediate and stir the outcome towards a broadly acceptable consensus, which will be acceptable to the IGC. The Union will continue to develop and with future changes in the national and international political, economic and/or security spheres it is also expectable that the EU will sooner or later face the need for further changes in its constitutional order. If this Convention on the Future of the Union will live up to its full potential by effectively producing Europe's first constitution, the 'Convention-model' could provide an efficient new model to solve institutional and constitutional challenges still laying ahead.

Notes

[1] Research Officer at the Federal Trust. I gratefully acknowledge the support and consistent feedback from Jo Shaw and also the very helpful suggestions and comments from Lynn Dobson. I would also like to thank Anna Verges Bausili, Sebastian Barnutz, Alexis Krachai and David Fines for commenting on earlier drafts of the paper.

[2] http://European-convention.eu.int/pdf/LKNEN.pdf

[3] http://European-convention.eu.int/docs/speeches/1.pdf

[4] Lodge, 1998: 347.

[5] Yataganas, 2001: 13.

[6] For example tax policy for the British government or trade policy for the French government. The smaller states were categorically opposed to giving up 'their' one Commissioner per member state.

[7] http://www.cec.org.uk/info/pubs/bbriefs/bb/19.htm; Monar and Wessels (eds), 2001.

[8] Presidency Conclusions, Nice European Council Meeting, 7, 8 and 9 December 2000, paragraph II, Press Release: Brussels (8/12/2000) No: 400/1/00; Presidency Conclusion, Helsinki European Council, 10 and 11 December 1999, Press Release: Brussels (11/12/1999) No: 00300/1/99; Presidency Conclusion, Cologne European Council Meeting, 3 and 4 June 1999, paragraph IV, CFSP Presidency Statement: Cologne (4/6/1999) – Press Release No: 150/99.

[9] Lodge, 1998: 351.

[10] See also Yataganas, 2001: 6.

[11] BBC news, 30 January, 2001, Franco-German alliance 'still special', http://news.bbc.co.uk/1/hi/world/europe/1144562.stm; Yataganas, 2001: 36.

[12] See also Wessels, 'Nice Results 2001 and Gunter Pleuger 2001: 9.

[13] Christiansen and Jørgensen, 1998: 450.

[14] Yataganas, 2001.

[15] Lodge, 1998: 349.

[16] Straw, 2001.

[17] Giscard d'Estaing, 2002a.

[18] Declaration on the Future of the Union, 2001.

[19] Ibid.

[20] Ibid.

[21] Ibid.

[22] *Die Presse*, 2002.

[23] *EU Observer*, 2001.

[24] *EU Observer*, 2002.

[25] CONV 369/02.

[26] CONV 528/03

[27] Interestingly, the Convention's timeframe has been extended so that the final document can now be expected by June 2003. Yet, this change has been informally decided by the Convention itself rather than the heads of European governments.

[28] European Parliament, Lamassoure Report.

[29] *Der Kurier*, 2002.

[30] See House of Commons, 2002a and House of Commons 2002b.

[31] Declaration on the Future of the Union, 2001: 25.

[32] Germany has now sent Joschka Fischer, France has sent Dominique de Villepin, Greece has sent Giorgios Papendreou.

[33] Declaration on the Future of the Union, 2001.

[34] Pernice has suggested such a two part treaty in Pernice, 2002; see also CONV 250.

[35] Magnette, 2002.

[36] http://www.fedtrust.co.uk/conferences.htm; *Le Monde* 2002a and *Le Monde* 2002b.

[37] The only exceptions would be the two Commission representatives, who have been nominated to their position rather than elected, and a few government representatives who are not formally part of their national governments, like the German government representative Peter Glotz who is a university professor in Switzerland.

[38] Bond, 2002.

[39] Lodge, 1998: 348.

Rethinking the methods of dividing and exercising powers in the EU Reforming subsidiarity, national parliaments and legitimacy

Anna Vergés Bausili[1]

Introduction

With some changes in the actual formulation of the mandate, both the Nice and Laeken European Councils put at the top of the post-Nice process of reflection and Treaty revision the consideration of a more precise delimitation of powers between the EU and its member states.[2] Various issues are behind this rather broad mandate: *inter alia* a search for clarity as for 'who does what'; a perception of creeping competence; an attempt to appease critical public opinion; a search for better appraisals as to when and how the Community should intervene; and an overall search for legitimacy.

Thus, among other likely changes in the Treaty, the principle of subsidiarity is very likely to be reformed. The changes in its current conception (as defined by Maastricht and Amsterdam) appear as largely procedural – which nonetheless might affect and extend the substantial scope of the principle. If the IGC confirms these proposals, national parliaments will for the first time enter the domain of EU law and policy-making with a specific remit: the monitoring of the application of subsidiarity by European institutions.[3] Although the introduction of national parliaments into the EU system is broadly a desirable change, the actual format of that entry, and the considerations on which it rests, deserve full consideration.

While the debate on subsidiarity is gradually shifting away from the competence context into the legitimacy agenda, this paper will aim first of all, at placing and assessing the role of subsidiarity within the wider context of a *problematic* EU competence system, and secondly, it will look at various aspects relating to charging national parliaments to monitor subsidiarity. Thus, a first section will aim at painting the contours of the current system and some problematic aspects against the mandate of delimiting powers; second, it will evaluate subsidiarity as a solution; and thirdly, it will look at controversial aspects of the solutions proposed by the Convention.

The *problematic* EU competence system and the limits of the Nice and Laeken 'delimitation' mandate

Any consideration of the notion of subsidiarity ought to start from and be based upon an assessment of the nature of the EU system of competence as it stands, and upon a broad understanding of its peculiar nature.

The first point to emphasise about the EU system of powers is its complexity. In the EU competence system, political, legal and institutional dynamics interact aiming to produce an overall balance between national and Community interests. In addition, policy dynamics, legal provisions, institutions and values all combine to shape and define outcomes.

The EU competence system is more than a listing of transferred or attributed powers: it involves systemic and sub-systemic dynamics. Rather than being designed as a classic public international organisation, the EU was devised to generate a practice of common governance, where the division of powers is played out at the sub-systemic level. Indeed, the governance of its policies, the nature of procedures (whether intergovernmental or Community) and the various decision-making arrangements (whether requiring unanimity or QMV) determine in *de facto* terms the division of competences between the EU and member states.

Although the principle by which EU powers are attributed is central to the system, the statement of the principle says very little about the actual operation (and also evolution) of the system. In truth, the EU powers have evolved over the years through a succession of Treaty revisions (IGCs) where, through interstate bargaining of various preferences and relative power, EU powers have been altered.[4] Yet, not only has the primacy of the rule of intergovernmental attribution been challenged over the years on various fronts, it is also the case that the 'governance' aspects of attributed powers have proven their significance alongside the 'high politics' of IGCs. The input of governments' preferences and power is central, particularly at Treaty reform stages, yet one cannot deny the existence of processes well beyond either the strictly intergovernmental attribution of competences or agency/ delegation structures which reside in the political praxis and the legal and institutional arrangements for the operation of the system. In fact, one can argue that the mechanisms of jurisdictional attribution have over the years mutated towards a more institutional rather than intergovernmental model, that is, where (besides the resorting to IGCs to increase formal powers) demands from and responses within the system have become dynamic forces for the expansion of the competence system itself. Without attempting to enter into theoretical analyses, the purpose here is simply to consider the assumptions made in the Nice and Laeken mandate for a clear delimitation of powers, and subsequently, to assess the role of the principle of subsidiarity in the context of the problematic competence system.

A largely limitless competence system and the sub-systemic governance processes

EU powers are attributed, but that attribution is peculiar in many respects. Attribution of powers itself has, over the years, lost its 'enumerative' and limited character.[5] As an international organisation, of course, EU powers are conferred by member states (Article 5 EC Treaty);[6] yet the EU displays a practice of intergovernmental attribution of powers far from the classic international mould. Although originally a 'contractual' approach to Community competence was adopted, and this approach was confirmed by the Court in early cases,[7] already by the early 1960s, the original conception based on the primacy of an explicit attribution of powers, had eroded in some quarters: notably, the major challenge to the limitative and enumerative character of attribution being the doctrine of implied powers as developed by the Court of Justice. In other words, according to the Court, powers would be implied in favour of the Community where they were considered necessary in order to serve legitimate ends pursued by it under the Treaty. Indeed, from the teleological approach to competence of the Court, the Community *extended* the *scope* of attributed powers.[8]

Subsequently, over the early 1970s and 1980s the extended recourse to Article 308 EC (ex. 235) made by the Council on the basis of 'unmatching' objectives and actual means, *extending* and *expanding* Community competence into new policy areas, meant a further blow to the original intergovernmental contractual approach to competence. To start with, expansion occurred away from resort to IGCs i.e. within the system; but also as the Community expanded its competence into new policy areas and the single market programme started to unfold, the limits of the classic enumeration principle on which attribution of Community powers originally had rested, started to be less and less significant.

In sum, substantial jurisdictional changes have occurred without being the result of actual Treaty amendments, but rather originating at the sub-systemic level i.e. in the operation of the system, or triggered by its institutions. Or in other words, the institutional system and its policies do not seem a neutral or passive factor, but rather influence interests and demands on the system.[9]

The institutions' power of autonomous organisation

Intergovernmental attribution has also been challenged by the capacity of EU institutions to work autonomously and, linked to the functional delimitation of powers and the institutional balance of powers in the EU, the institutions' power of autonomous organisation has been conducive to material expansion of competences,[10] or to the development of new policy directions.[11]

In the context of the work of EU institutions – which, *de jure* and in practice, are autonomous – the values, beliefs, norms and identities embedded in them shape events. Indeed, the Treaty imposes *obligations* on Community institutions to pursue Treaty objectives (particularly on the Commission for its power of initiative to pursue the general interest). Policy initiative is not only entrenched in the Treaty (Article 211 EC) but is also coloured by intra-institutional values and culture. The Commission has assumed the role of defender of the Community interest and has often proclaimed its 'duty' to submit proposals, to explore and launch policy initiatives at its own discretion, independently and irrespective of the existence or not of a legal base. Where those objectives are defined in wide functional terms (as in the context of programmes such as the pursuit of EMU or the single market), the room for autonomous policy activism has been larger. Indeed, the Commission has historically triggered policy dossiers justifying Community involvement on the grounds of pursuing the attainment of objectives of the Treaty and the operation itself of the single market. Clearly, Treaty objectives (particularly when generally defined) do not confer competence, yet in the past, the search for a legal base has by no means been an insurmountable hurdle preventing policy initiative. In brief, although general objectives do not imply the power on the Community to act, the Commission has often interpreted competences deriving from tasks and purposes and, in a good number of cases, its policy leadership has been significant.

To recapitulate, the institutions' power of autonomous organisation has in some cases been the determining factor in the expansion and extension of Community powers. The Commission has historically pushed the material limits of EU competence through its power of initiative and its privileged presence at Council tables, but with not less radical consequences, the ECJ's favouring of a teleological rather than a classic international public law approach, has developed the doctrine of implied powers, has established the supremacy and direct effect of Community law and has constitutionalised the Treaties.[12]

A multi-layered competence system

The current division of EU powers no longer concerns solely the national executives and the European institutions. The EU system relies on the sub-national levels of government for a very good deal of its policies. Not only sub-national authorities implement and manage structural policies and various Community programmes, but in countries where territorial units hold legislative powers the transposition of Community legislation into domestic law is a matter for decentralised authorities. Indeed, although Community law-making powers can be more easily demarcated, policy-making in the EU and also programme based policy (such as regional policy, environmental policy etc.) is more multi-layered and unbound – where the separation between national and European arenas has eroded, and governments' gate-keeping power appears as a thing of the past.[13] Indeed, not only is the policy arena permeable to policy networks of interest and pressure groups,[14] but also sub-national authorities mobilise and input policy and law-making.[15] The result is a complex and 'messy' policy and law-making process with a good degree of random, irrational and unintended effects.[16]

In sum, the implementation of the Nice and Laeken European Council mandates to attain a better delimitation of powers between the EU and the member states should not forget that Community powers permeate through member states' structures. In this context the mandate for a clear delimitation of powers *between EU and the member states* can only be treated with caution.

A malleable competence system with frail buffers

The EU competence system is one that facilitates the development of further material co-operation when there is sufficient political will. The problems of the system are largely rooted in its horizontally defined terms. The functional approach to competence, the possibility to expand the range of common actions through Article 308, the 'relaxation' of national control in adopting legislation through QMV, and in particular, the lack of strict legal and/or political limits to competence development are substantial features of the system. These features (accompanied with vertical democratic aspects – on which more later) have led to concerns about 'creeping competence'. Three types of situations are usually identified under this title: the adoption of unjustified/unwanted legislation under QMV procedures, expansion of material competence under Article 308, and EU legislation entering domains where the Community has no explicitly attributed powers.

Firstly, Treaty provisions on the approximation of laws for the purposes of the operation of an internal market (Articles 94, 95 EC) are broad and limitless and particularly sensitive in conditions of QMV decision-making. In addition, as the Treaty does not explain the *principles* governing the exercise of attributed competences (apart from the principle of subsidiarity) the limits of EU intervention are perceived as being rather loose, in fact, rather uncertain. Indeed, no guidance, apart from a general pledge to act in accordance with the two conditions of subsidiarity and proportionality is at hand.[17] Furthermore, the institutional guarantees of compliance with the division of competences are perceived as inadequate (with the Community over-regulating and intervening where it should not). In addition, since the mid 1980s, as the single market programme gradually unfolded, the public perception of interference, over-regulation and intrusion has grown considerably.

Secondly, although the principle of attributed powers (Article 5(1)) boils down to the requirement of legal basis for each EU act i.e. the identification of legal base, it does not appear intrinsically difficult in the EU to find a legal base to launch initiatives; in other words, competence expansion truly resides in the collection of sufficient political will. Article 308 has been used in close to 700 instances by the Council acting unanimously, and thus, given sufficient (unanimous) political acceptance, the EU system allows for the launching of initiatives as need arises. In short, even though recently the Court has adopted a firmer stance (tobacco case), the limits to Community co-operation are mainly political, not legal, and as Article 308 requires unanimity, it has often been the political will of governments which has been the key to go beyond Treaty provisions. Creeping has in some cases been unintended (the same intergovernmental dynamics have led to unwanted effects, and there have been a few cases of clear supranational drive), but often creeping has occurred with the acceptance of national governments. In sum, it holds true (not only through Article 308, but also through sectoral provisions and also outside the Community pillar) that where there is sufficient political will, there is a (legal) way.

Thirdly, the intervention of the Community has been particularly contested in areas of 'complementary competence' i.e. in areas in which the intervention by the Community is limited to supplementing, supporting, or co-ordinating the action of the member states.[18] In these areas, although the Treaty lays down a negative delimitation of competence, such as excluding legislative harmonisation, Community intervention is to be limited to executive provisions, and it cannot have the effect of pre-empting or excluding intervention by the member states – who retain the power to adopt legislative rules.

In sum, objective-based Community intervention has meant availability for the legislator of legal bases to launch actions from a variety of policy fields which could be justifiable for the ultimate purpose to be attained. In these cases there have been occasional abuses of the principle of subsidiarity (sometimes under QMV arrangements, sometimes with full governmental consent) and of the principle of proportionality in the attempt to ensure full compliance from all member states.

No 'external' (democratic) control of competence matters

The question of whether the Treaties do (or do not) confer competence on the Union to act in a specific case, and to what extent the subsidiarity principle is being complied with, is a political judgement that rests largely on the Community institutions participating in the legislative process – and in fact, only on some.[19] Indeed, monitoring of the compliance with jurisdictional limits is for the most part exercised by the institutions of the Union. Although the Commission and the European Parliament have traditionally been in favour of growth in EU powers, the Council has been not less disrespectful.[20] The Committee of the Regions and the Economic and Social Committee, as consultative rather than legislative bodies, do not hold any advisory role in competence matters. However, they can and do raise subsidiarity concerns within their advisory legislative capacity or through own-initiative opinions.

Thus external bodies (national parliaments, regional parliaments, public opinion) have been outsiders on competence matters, and have been able to influence and control the EU competence system to the extent that they have managed to input decision-making either in an informal manner, or by controlling the positions adopted by their governments' representatives in the Council. Generally speaking, governments have taken advantage of insufficient involvement by national and regional parliaments in EU competence matters and, to a good degree, they have benefited from screening out domestic scrutiny and opposition. Expansion of material competence through Article 308 (as opposed to via IGCs) has been convenient in avoiding domestic scrutiny.

There is, however, another sense in which external control of competence matters is lacking. Through the doctrine of the unity in the representation of the state before European institutions, government executives have gained control on competences outside their remit, or on powers which were devolved. At the same time, neither regional levels of government, nor the Committee of the Regions can act against encroachment. There is little possibility of review by the European Court of Justice of the competence question as national parliaments and regional authorities do not have standing at present to bring direct actions for the annulment of EU measures before the Court. But, furthermore, the European Court of Justice's review capacity under Article 230 is largely procedural in nature, as the Court has repeatedly considered subsidiarity as ultimately a political appraisal as to which level is best to carry out a public function. That is, subsidiarity is justiciable on the grounds of observance to legal bases or otherwise in recourse, in an *ex post* basis, to Article 230 where annulment of decisions can be brought before the Court on the grounds of the rights of institutions in EU decision making processes not being fully respected.

In sum, there is no direct external control on the political appraisals involved in competence attribution (through Article 308) nor in the exercise of attributed competence; and in addition, there is no judicial remedy for encroachment of regional competences.

To recapitulate, the EU competence system is complex and peculiar in many respects. Attribution of powers occurs by explicit conferrals resulting from intergovernmental dynamics but it is influenced just as much by the nature of the institutional, legal and organisational set up of the system. Thus the EU competence system is in fact a rather plastic matter which, rather than being definable by intergovernmental attribution of powers, is evolving and played-out institutionally through different methods and procedures at the governance level. Indeed, although the system is based on the express intergovernmental attribution of powers, the system is largely defined in horizontal terms and has its own mechanisms to develop, extend and expand competence, which have shaped the system's evolution. Neither the intergovernmental nor the governance levels are impermeable, independent from each other or water-tight.

The importance of the governance level, the functional multi-disciplinary approach to competence, the autonomous capacity of its institutions and its flexible legal arrangements to permit further integration (where political will exists) have all contributed to a system of powers which is easily expandable and evolving as new needs appear. Yet the competence system with its flexible and plastic qualities is problematic in at least two major senses: it has no significant qualitative limits, and its democratic control is insufficient. Indeed, the system appears as largely limitless *ratione materiae*, but more importantly, the control of its limits and its management is inadequate. As the EU is a peculiar and complex system, the methods of dividing and controlling competence shifts in the EU (but also competence sharing) will consequently have to be fit to the double challenge.

In addition, public opinion has, since the early 1990s, gradually come to perceive the competence system as expanding in an unconditional and almost unstoppable fashion; or in other words, the political appraisals involved in competence attribution and competence-sharing have gradually become a matter of public concern. With this strong background of public hostility the Nice and Laeken Declarations called for a clear delimitation of powers between the EU and the member states. To what extent is the search for legal certainty in the EU competence system chimerical? Where delimitation means clarification of the competence system, some actions can be put into place to attain some transparency – such as explicitly specifying that the EU is an evolving system and a structure that permits common governance, classifying competences into categories, defining the meaning of exclusive/shared/complementary competences, making provisions more readable, etc. Where beyond clarification, delimitation of powers means setting limits to Community involvement, the system could not be changed into one incorporating a rigid demarcation of powers unless this occurred at the cost of restraining future evolution and flexibility.[21] In sum, the competence system has frail buffers and lacks democratic control and, at least in this sense, there is need for reform. In addition, political appraisals on competence attribution and competence sharing (as most Community powers are shared powers) are no longer matters capable of being kept away from public scrutiny. But, to what extent is the principle of subsidiarity, as currently operational, a solution in the context of the various problematic aspects of the EU competence system?

The subsidiarity solution: which kind of solution?

As a response to the peculiarities of the EU competence system, subsidiarity accommodates to the functional, open, evolving and dynamic nature of the EU polity.

Subsidiarity in the EU is not, however, a substantive principle guiding decisions as to what is the best level to allocate powers. Substantial allocation of powers is dealt with at the highest intergovernmental level where subsidiarity, as a normative principle, does not apply. Subsidiarity applies only in the exercise of conferred powers either shared or complementary, and it does not have force to review or challenge the *acquis communautaire*, nor the Commission's right of initiative.

Although there is no direct link between subsidiarity and QMV, as the use of qualified majority voting increases, subsidiarity acts as a principle of political restraint in the EU in that it requires that proposed actions falling under the sphere of shared powers must be those which cannot be achieved by member states alone, or can be better achieved by the Community (due to the scale or effects). In brief, subsidiarity cannot prevent states being outnumbered in the Council but it can set, in areas of non-exclusive competence, material limits to the horizontal nature of Community competence.[22] Subsidiarity, rather than a normative principle (as to what is the *best* level of action on the grounds of efficiency and proximity to the citizen), is a political appraisal on the *need* of policy or law-making at EU level, and on the value added of Community action under attributed shared powers.

Concerning the problematic institutional autonomy, subsidiarity is applied differently by each of the European institutions but, basically, subsidiarity is, across institutions, a catch-phrase for legislative and policy restraint. In practice, legislative and policy restraint is translated, under the Amsterdam Protocol on the application of the principle of subsidiarity,[23] in the obligation for the Commission to proceed to wide internal and external consultations before formal proposals are made, to justify each proposal in the preambles of its documents,[24] and to ensure that financial and administrative impact of new proposals is kept to a minimum.[25] Subsidiarity, in the sense of a better assumption and application of the principle by institutions, can provide a remedy for abuses of power of initiative. However, the perception of a hyper-active Commission and Court is to a substantial extent exaggerated. A change in Commissions' attitudes has been underway since the late 1980s and the early 1990s.[26] Indeed, after a period of large legislative activity (part of the internal market programme), successive Commissions have moved to a 'do less but do better' approach. Not only have proposals been withdrawn, but also quantitatively fallen since the 1990s[27]. In addition, the Commission has entered an almost 'apologetic' phase where not only it claims that it has reduced the number of legislative proposals, but also claims that it consults widely before submitting a proposal. In other words, not only cultural and institutional values matter, but also the socio-political environment does condition institutional activism – and the post-Danish ratification period is one of policy restraint. Furthermore, while a better implementation and monitoring of subsidiarity is instrumental as a device to monitor abuses, the respect of subsidiarity and proportionality should also be considered as regards the legislator. The Commission claims that its duty to submit proposals has come to be aggravated by legislative pressure from other institutions, interest and pressure groups; and also Council and EP have increased their submissions of detailed draft proposals. Indeed, according to Grevi, about 80 per cent of proposals over the last ten years have been tabled by invitation of the Council or member states, and as he notes, 'domestic politics are perhaps more relevant to this debate than the balance of powers in Europe'.[28] Proportionality has not always been respected by the legislators either.[29] In sum, if power of initiative is a source of creeping competence one has to recognise that *de facto* (policy and legal) initiative is not exercised alone by the Commission.

As a normative principle, subsidiarity (as currently defined) has little value. The democratic value of the current understanding of subsidiarity rests solely on an absolute and general assumption that governance by member states is more democratic than governance by EU institutions. Although there is a fundamental difference between the principle as it appears in the (non-binding) preamble and its definition in Article 5(2) EC and in the Protocol on subsidiarity appended to the Amsterdam Protocol,[30] as a postulate, subsidiarity applies solely to the actions of European institutions. Indeed, while the preamble of the Treaty refers to the democratic principle of governance as close as possible to the citizen, Article 5 and the Protocol place subsidiarity as a principle to set limits to Community involvement, and it is applied as putting the burden of proof on the Community to justify involvement, while guiding solely the relationship between Community and the member states. Subsidiarity understands the EU polity as a classic intergovernmental organisation governing competence conflicts between Community and national institutions. Its application not only ignores the multi-level nature of Community actions but deliberately avoids entering into the actual exercise and implementation of EU law and policy. By choosing not to enter into intra-national divisions of powers the principle of subsidiarity means an effective bias towards national centralisation and, not surprisingly, subsidiarity is silent on central governments' encroachment on regional prerogatives – and even in contradiction with the framework of the constitutional system in various member states. Thus, while regions with legislative power have *obligations* within the legislative work of the Union i.e. they are responsible for converting EU directives into their own legislation, and also responsible for implementing EU policies in all areas falling within their legislative remit,[31] their capacity to influence policy and law-making in the areas where they hold legislative competence has been curtailed.

Overall, subsidiarity offers a flexible response to the broad, facilitative expanding nature of the EU system but (as it is applied today) it has no broad normative value. As the EU defines its objectives in functional and broad terms, and as it is the gathering of sufficient political will that determines the limits of Community involvement, subsidiarity takes due notice of the dynamic nature of the system and works in a preventive manner as a way to counterbalance the horizontal limitless and evolving nature of the EU competence system. Subsidiarity consists of a political assessment of the virtues of Community intervention (which can be made from a variety of senses) in a system facilitating common ventures. By setting material limits to the involvement of the Community in the exercise of shared powers subsidiarity is intended as a jurisdictional safeguard against functional creeping. As a political judgement subsidiarity cannot bring legal certainty to the EU competence system; rather, subsidiarity will act upon institutional activism, upon broad legal bases, upon intervention into complementary competences, and overall, setting buffers to the expansive character of the system.

Yet, the constitutional challenge is to design a system which builds on the *sui generis* character of the EU system of powers, and is more transparent, and allows evolution but, last and not least, that is more democratic. Under current arrangements, the use of subsidiarity is being monitored by European institutions alone. The deeper democratic problem underlying the EU competence system is not only the encroachment of constitutional rights of some regions with legislative power, but the insufficient accountability of governments and European institutions in political decisions regarding *division* and *exercise* of competences.

Besides some pros and cons of the principle, subsidiarity deficiencies are deceptively over-stated and to a large extent victims of misperception. It has been estimated that in 5 per cent of cases of legislation, the Community has trespassed the limits as to what was necessary or better achieved by the Community.[32] Yet at the same time, and although it has been quantified as only a 5 per cent of cases where subsidiarity and proportionality have not been observed, pervasive public perception is that the proportion is higher and Community action is too intrusive. The Court itself has never found a violation of the principle of subsidiarity by legislative actions of the Community.[33] The notion of subsidiarity is also overused by using it as a catch-phrase or reassuring measure for hostile public opinion's perceptions of creeping federalism. See for instance the link between the UK government shift towards accepting an EU Constitution and the emphasis put on subsidiarity as a counterbalance to what eurosceptic public opinion would perceive as another leap forward.[34]

In conclusion, the principle of subsidiarity does play a role in the EU competence system as a form of setting limits to the exercise of multi-disciplinary policy and law-making powers. The principle suffers from over-publicity, and its role is partial if not minimal in the context of the broader problematic aspects of the EU competence system (such as the ever increasing resort to QMV, legal uncertainty, the unchecked use of Article 308, encroachment of sub-national powers, supervision of political decisions regarding the exercise of shared competences, etc). The reform of subsidiarity has a point, but necessarily it will have to be as a part of a larger package involving other possible amendments to the Treaties which the Convention is looking at such as a categorisation of EU competences, clarifying the distinction between general objectives and actual powers, a clarification of EU legal instruments, inserting a declaration that powers which have not been attributed to the EU are national powers (as in the German Constitution), defining material limits to EU power (through negative competence provisions)[35] in various complementary competences, amending Article 308, etc.

Thus what is really at stake in the EU competence system as a whole, and in the notion of subsidiarity in particular, relates to the politics of competence shifts and competence sharing. In fact, as most EU powers are shared powers, the Nice and Laeken mandate for a clearer delimitation may be deceptive. Besides the worthy aim of clarity, strengthening a *partnership* model (rather than clear demarcation of 'who does what') appears as a more appropriate departure point and democratic way to address the division and exercise of powers in the EU. Indeed, the EU institutional system itself does not rest on the traditional separation of powers but, rather, the Treaties sketch a system where institutions, national and Community, co-operate. One can add that as volume of legislation has been decreasing and Community intervention becomes 'softer', partnership at all stages of law-making becomes more important to the attainment of pursued objectives.[36] Subsidiarity has a role in this context and its reform is desirable in direction to its normative credentials, that is, in the sense that decisions ought to be made as close as possible to the citizens, but also that those decisions on competence and its exercise are to be more democratically conducted. That is particularly so as the political appraisals on attribution and exercise of competences are increasingly contested within the member states. Competence sensitivity calls for the opening up of those political decisions concerning which is the best level for action.

The Convention work on the reform of subsidiarity: the meeting of the two agendas of subsidiarity and the role of national parliaments

The Convention approached the range of issues involved in the delimitation of competences with the creation of three Working Groups (WG): one concerning the delimitation of complementary competences, another concerning the role of national parliaments and, finally, one focusing on the principle of subsidiarity as such. None of the WGs drafted concrete articles. WGs reported to the Convention; and the Praesidium and the Secretariat interpreted the views expressed in the WGs and translated them into actual draft articles.

While the principle of subsidiarity is an important part of the broader discussion on EU competence delimitation, the WG on subsidiarity limited its mandate to examining how the compliance with the principle (as currently defined and applied from the guidelines of the Subsidiarity Protocol) could be enhanced and also monitored by either a judicial or political type of procedure. In other words, the WG on subsidiarity did not consider subsidiarity as a constitutional principle nor did it question its scope as spelled out by the Protocol on Subsidiarity – as adopted at the Amsterdam Treaty review. Instead, it focussed on reviewing its implementation. Proportionality was also largely left aside of the deliberations of the WG on subsidiarity. The broader mandate for a clarification of competences was addressed by the WG on complementary competences which recommended that a clearer division of powers could be attained by a combination of various amendments: firstly, the insertion of a new title in the Constitutional Treaty dealing with powers, where both the fundamental principles of the system and the different types of Union action would be spelled out. In addition, the WG proposed the amendment of Article 308, of Articles 94-95, a rephrasing of the statement on 'ever closer union', a definition of 'complementary competences', and the need for a hierarchy of legislative acts and instruments. The WG however did not propose concrete wording of these provisions. The WG on the role of national parliaments took as its task to examine scrutiny at the national level comparatively, whether national parliaments could/should have a role in controlling subsidiarity, and the role of national parliaments in the European architecture (examining the role of COSAC, increasing information flows, etc). Thus as the WG on complementary competences dealt with a basic, clear categorisation of EU actions and principles, the WG on subsidiarity did not deal with a substantial review of subsidiarity but with procedural reform. In other words, the terms of reference for the review of subsidiarity largely pre-empted the possibilities of substantial reform of the principle.

The single largest novelty on the reform of subsidiarity spelled out by this WG (and supported by the WG on the role for national parliaments and subsequently followed by the Praesidium's draft of the Protocol on the application of subsidiarity and proportionality[37]) consists of setting up an 'early warning system'. Through this procedural modification, alongside the main task of national parliaments to influence and to scrutinise their respective national executives, a new role was carved out for national parliaments to inspect directly the work of European institutions: namely the Commission and the legislators, as regards the exercise of Community powers (that is, shared and complementary).

Particularly as regards the scrutiny of European institutions the mechanism being proposed (the early warning system) is likely to be similar to the scrutiny system in force in the UK House of Commons:[38] notably, a rapid scrutiny and reporting consisting of sifting to identify documents of 'political or legal importance', with the capacity to raise 'reserves' on measures proposed.

The subsidiarity scrutiny performed by national parliaments will apply to all legislative proposals under co-decision and falling under the category of shared competences, but also to wide policy proposals such as Green Papers, White Papers, the Commission's Annual Work Programme, etc. It has also been proposed to apply to other draft texts such as proposals under a reformed Article 308.

The subsidiarity scrutiny will be largely a task of sifting proposals on the grounds of subsidiarity rather than policy merits, as is currently the case in the UK House of Commons. In other words, the subsidiarity scrutiny is not to enter into the substance (i.e. policy choices) of the proposals, but will solely assess whether subsidiarity and proportionality have been adequately respected by the Commission and (indirectly) by the Council and European Parliament. Should national parliaments individually consider that such respect has not been fully honoured, they will have the right to raise a warning directly to the Commission or indirectly to the legislators. Depending on the number of warnings raised by national parliaments, the Commission/ legislators will be obliged to reconsider, redraft or withdraw the draft proposal under consideration. Parliaments will have six weeks to give a reasoned opinion on the subsidiarity aspects of Community proposals (which seems sufficient, as the current scrutiny system in the UK normally allows less time). Finally, a limited litigation channel is proposed to be opened to those parliaments which believe their opinions have not been duly considered. How final decisions (on the subsidiarity and proportionality of Community proposals) are reached domestically and, particularly, how to reach single positions in countries with bicameral systems is a matter left for domestic political settlement.

The Convention has considered various options as to how and when national parliaments would input the legislative process in order to consider subsidiarity aspects. First, national parliaments are to receive legislative proposals directly from the Commission. Second, within six weeks of the transmission date, national parliaments are to be entitled to issue a reasoned opinion on the proposal (or an aspect of it) concerning subsidiarity (and not the substance of the proposal). Depending on the number of objections, the legislator is to give further reasoning for the necessity of the act, or the Commission would re-examine its proposal (meaning either a withdrawal, an amendment or the maintenance of the proposal). Thirdly, proposals were made in the first drafts for the involvement of national parliaments at the final stages of the co-decision procedure, that is national parliaments would be able to assess subsidiarity considerations at the time of the convening of the Conciliation Committee and thus examine the Council's common position and amendments introduced by the European Parliament.

The scrutiny by national parliaments, beyond the establishment of an early warning procedure, is also to include the possibility of calling Commissioners to give oral evidence in the national parliaments, and is expected to take on board other proposals being made in the Commission White Paper on Governance, such as the inclusion of 'subsidiarity sheets' looking at the justification for Community intervention – rather than its substantial or policy contents.

But what will the subsidiarity scrutiny involve? The principle of attribution entails that the Community can only act if power to act has been expressly conferred to the Community by member states – in other words, when appropriate legal base exists for the Community to act. Judgements on the legal basis of proposals (although they are political in the sense that legal base may condition institutional balance), are ultimately objective legal appraisals, and discrepancies can be resolved through resort to the European Court Justice (Article 230 EC). Subsidiarity judgements however go beyond legal base considerations, in fact, they do not refer to the existence of competence, but entail a substantial political judgement on the adequacy of any

level to attain more efficiently and democratically whatever objectives pursued.

In the early warning system prototype, national parliaments are not to consider matters of content of the proposals, but only subsidiarity considerations. But one could wonder how easily substantive issues can be separated from subsidiarity and proportionality considerations for, in fact, subsidiarity involves political judgements as to what is the best level of action. Can a sifting through the contents of a proposal in order to identify added value and benefits of Community level action be made without entering into policy choices? In short, to what extent are subsidiarity and substance not related?

The Commons' scrutiny system provides some clues on the type and scope of scrutiny proposed. If a similar model is followed, firstly, a legal analysis would examine the legal bases invoked in drafting proposals and/or review options made in the choice of legal base by the Commission, and/or scrutinise the Commission's (or the legislators') assertions of power to act.[39] As mentioned before, however, the appraisals of legal bases are ultimately judicial and relatively uncontroversial. The most problematic aspect relates to the political argumentation on the need for Community action and its added value. Here the drafters of the early warning system insist on one point: national parliaments are not to become co-legislators. In other words, a distinction is being insisted upon: that is, a distinction between judgements on substance and judgements of subsidiarity; or in other terms, between appraisals of policy merits and appraisals on subsidiarity. So, could simply *unwanted* legislation (under QMV for instance or 'unwanted' on policy grounds) be stopped on the grounds of subsidiarity? The answer will have to be no. Also the criteria to define what is beyond the limits ought not to question attributed powers, nor decision-making procedures, but only unnecessary or unjustifiable Community intervention in areas of shared or complementary competence, or otherwise disproportionate intervention (on the grounds of the principle of proportionality). In other terms, either with or without the consent of all member states i.e. under QMV arrangements, only the legislation which appears as dubiously justifiable for Community action, or interfering in areas of complementary competence, could be challenged by national parliaments under the early warning system.

Thus on the nature of the political appraisals of subsidiarity, the opinions by national parliaments are likely to echo the pre-legislative consultation stages, that is, national parliaments' reasoned opinions are to consider not the policy choices made, but to argue the added value of Community intervention and/or intensity questions – that is, proportionality. In other words, national parliaments will be listened to on questions such as the impact of proposals, likely effectiveness, cost, consistency or result of a proposed Community measure.[40] Parliaments therefore will be given the right to question European institutions' reasoning on the latter, and although they will not be requested to express a view on the merits of the proposal (for they are not co-legislators), their opinion will indicate *indirectly* their concern or approval on the contents. These concerns, in turn, are likely to be tinted by domestic cultural and socio-economic values.

The limited scope of subsidiarity inquiries seems to also rest on the fact that, should substantial assessments be conducted, evidence would have to be gathered thus overloading the tasks of national parliamentarians and departmental committees. In this sense, the observations made by UK MPs in favour of current scrutiny procedures in the UK are totally relevant to the early warning system scrutiny:

> 'The main reasons for not paying more attention to the merits are that far more evidence would have to be gathered, making our task unmanageable, it would be difficult or impossible for a cross-party committee to reach agreement on documents which address issues of party political controversy, and we could duplicate the work of Departmental Select Committees (DSCs) and European Standing Committees. (…) A more comprehensive examination of merits would require a radical reorganisation of the scrutiny system – for example splitting the European Scrutiny Committee into a number of committees (or sub-committees) which combined the functions of the Scrutiny Committee and the Standing Committees, each responsible for several departments. However, in a system such as that, committees would often find it impossible to agree on the merits of documents, they would have heavy workloads covering a range of departments, and there would be a continuous risk of overload with the work of DSCs. Greater involvement of DSCs in EU matters, thereby integrating consideration of EU and UK policy and bringing specialist knowledge to bear on it, is a better option if it can be achieved.'[41]

Time constraints, the scarcity of human resources and overload will determine the quality of subsidiarity checks conducted by national parliaments. However, the performing of the scrutiny of subsidiarity by national parliaments should not involve a radical overhaul of parliamentary structures and procedures, as the scope of the subsidiarity checks does not require examination of contents.

A number of other controversial issues are also on the table. Preliminary drafts of the early warning system rightly acknowledged that subsidiarity and proportionality breaches are not exclusive to the Commission. Therefore, warnings ought to amount to a political call both for a review of proposals by the Commission College, and for amendments by the Council and the European Parliament. Indeed, even if the early warning system is, at its minimum, an information exercise, it is nonetheless likely to affect policy initiative as well as affect informal practices such as conciliation arrangements between European Parliament and Council.[42] Would the intervention by national parliaments be allowed to unravel the hard fought positions during the conciliation phase? Moreover, it is likely to change relations with the European Parliament, to involve changes to national parliamentary procedures, and have an effect on the variety of political cultures and values that underpin them across the EU member states. One cannot expect either that national parliaments will be neutral. In fact, they are very likely to be affected by domestic politics and reflect imbalances between national executives and parliaments.

In addition, what obligations should result from the national parliaments' views on the respect of subsidiarity and proportionality by the European institutions? National parliaments will gain a role of watchdogs consisting of a right to question Community institutions, and the right to issue warnings. Depending on the quantitative size of the warnings from national parliaments, the response by Community institutions can range from an obligation on the Commission to justify the proposals (where a small number of submissions have been made) to an outright re-examination of the proposals. Clearly, the warning is not proposed to amount to a veto as national parliaments are not co-legislators, and their mandatory powers will ultimately reside on their opinions being confirmed by the European Court of Justice – albeit on procedural grounds – or by member states' referrals to the Court. Indeed, broadening the right by national parliaments of resorting to the Court for judicial review (current Article 230) was a proposal made by the WG which was not welcome by various members of the Praesidium and the Convention, and indeed, it was not followed in either the first or the second draft of Protocol.[43] But beyond the litigant route, the defenders of the early warning system point out that the warnings will have their political teeth in their capacity to bring to the surface subsidiarity conflicts, and that they will oblige national and European institutions to confront subsidiarity considerations. National parliaments will not be able to propose amendments but solely to raise concerns on subsidiarity grounds, which entails an all-or-nothing power for national parliaments and with a possible right to withhold proposals in a similar sort of a 'scrutiny reserve resolution'.[44]

All in all, the early warning system confirms subsidiarity as a political judgement, and therefore not an appraisal to be made by Courts[45] – except insofar as providing legal remedies to breaches of the principle under certain procedure and conditions. The early warning system as designed by the WG on subsidiarity provided for resort to judicial review as a last resort mechanism for national parliaments claiming breaches of subsidiarity. The WG on subsidiarity foresaw the possibility of opening the list of privileged applicants on the basis of Article 230 to national parliaments. Nonetheless, the parliamentary resort to the Court is a possibility of appealing against violation of the principle of subsidiarity largely on procedural grounds.[46] The resort *ex-post* to the European Court of Justice therefore would not be on the grounds of contesting subsidiarity appraisals (as ultimately, it is understood that subsidiarity is a political judgement not susceptible to be undertaken by a judicial body) but a ruling on the legality of the procedures and respect of inter-institutional balances.

The WG made an attempt to minimise the political consequences of broadening the privilege to resorting to the Court by trying to make such a recourse limited and exceptional. Attempts to narrow down such a recourse to judicial proceedings for national parliaments were made by linking the right to final resort to the Court dependent on actions in an early phase. Equally, the proposal to grant a right of appeal to the Court of Justice for violation of the principle of subsidiarity to those regions which, within the framework of national institutional organisation, have legislative capacities, was ruled out. Rather, and on the procedural basis of Article 230, what was foreseen was merely the granting to the Committee of the Regions (rather than regional parliaments) the right to bring an action before the Court. This referral would relate to proposals submitted to the Committee of the Regions for an opinion and about which, in that opinion, it had expressed objections as regards compliance with early warning system procedures – rather than compliance with the principle of subsidiarity as such. The WG solely made the point that 'the European Court of Justice might in the future be prepared to look beyond the precise terms of the Treaty in defining the scope of judicial review where it perceives an insufficiency of legal protection, *inter alia* with regard to a perceived need to maintain the institutional balance'. Thus, as the scope of the judicial route is restricted, proposals have been made to broaden up the Protocol on Subsidiarity so that it includes a reference to 'local knowledge' and a 'margin of discretion'.[47] In other words, through changes in the Protocol and the reform of Article 230, one could preliminary ensure that regional prerogatives are not threatened. The respect of these prerogatives has also been attempted outside the umbrella of the principle of subsidiarity: notably, through the insertion of a statement concerning the respect of national identities and constitutional and political structures by the EU.

The Praesidium draft Protocols on Subsidiarity presented in late February 2003 and May 2003 did, however, make a choice for keeping the privileged access to the Court limited in cases of failure to comply with subsidiarity. Member states will bring to the Court actions for infringement of subsidiarity which may have been requested by national or regional parliaments, but ultimately, the scope for referral to the Court Praesidium is restricted to member states.

In sum, the major proposal on the table concerning subsidiarity proposes the setting up of an early warning system which would involve national parliaments in the political monitoring of the principle. A clear division of labour between national and European parliaments is made, and the early warning system squares a number of requirements. As its crafters argue, it avoids overburdening Community architecture with the creation of a new chamber or institution, it does not delay legislative processes and, in particular, it brings at the same time a larger role for national parliaments – which the Nice and Laeken Declarations also thought to achieve. Indeed, the early warning system has the potential to establish 'connection' and dialogue between national parliaments and European institutions. Irrespective of its various limitations, the early warning system entails a broadening of the political judgements of subsidiarity and the involvement of national parliaments in the EU policy and law-making process which appears as a positive development. The early warning system fails however at least in that it does not bring new normative grounds. The reform of subsidiarity is ultimately a procedural development in the *implementation* of the principle. It does not bring any further normative light into which rules ought to guide the exercise of Community competence. The reform of subsidiarity ought to have considered a redefinition of the concept: should democratic criteria (such as true proximity to citizen, margin of local discretion, respect of national constitutional arrangements) not be added into the criteria of scale and effect in Article 5 of the Treaty, the Protocol, or a future title on Union competences and actions?

Conclusions

The early warning system does not entail *per se* any radical overhaul of the notion of subsidiarity as understood in the EU since Maastricht and Amsterdam, but above all, it is a development of the underlying logic of subsidiarity as responding to the perception of 'competence creep'. Subsidiarity remains a principle guiding the exercise of shared and complementary powers, and an *instrument* to set material limits to Community intervention. While the major novelty concerns the entering into the subsidiarity procedures of national parliaments, the current reform of subsidiarity is likely to be limited to procedural changes in the examination of the *application* of the principle by European institutions and in the *monitoring* of compliance with it. Nonetheless, the effects of national parliaments overseeing subsidiarity considerations of both large policy programmes and individual legislative proposals are likely to be important. An increased sense of 'ownership' of European policy can develop in national parliaments as a result of the operation of the procedure. Ultimately, however, subsidiarity as a substantial principle remains unchanged. Indeed, on its normative side, subsidiarity in the EU remains an anyway thin constitutional concept which overlooks the multi-level nature of the EU polity, the value of the principle in the context of good governance and administration, and the prerogatives of regions with legislative powers.

In the current round of reform the major novelty in the notion of subsidiarity resides in its intersection with a parallel dossier: the role of national parliaments. This link between the two dossiers is the result of a context of increasing competence sensitivity where competence conflicts have become highly visible and controversial and, to a good degree, exaggerated. The contribution of the early warning system to the large complex and problematic nature of the EU competence system is clearly limited as, first, subsidiarity will not contribute to increased legal certainty on the EU competence system and, second, subsidiarity remains strongly padlocked to the European level. The current reform of subsidiarity rests on the understanding of subsidiarity as a political judgement, and is moving towards attaining a broader legitimisation of shifts and exercise of competence, namely by allowing a limited opening of those judgements involved on subsidiarity appraisals. Specially the political appraisals involved in the application of subsidiarity will be opened to scrutiny by national parliaments. In short, the early warning system can be more accurately pictured as a response to legitimacy concerns rather than to strictly competence issues.

Notes

[1] Research Officer at the Federal Trust. I would like to thank Jo Shaw, John Pinder, Martyn Bond and Lars Hoffmann for comments on earlier drafts.

[2] See the mandate to achieve a clearer delimitation of powers (as specified in Declaration 23 of the Treaty of Nice) and retaken by the Laeken Declaration (Annex I to Presidency Conclusions of European Council meeting at Laeken 14-15 December 2001 [SN 300/1/01 rev1]).

[3] National Parliaments have a say on treaty ratification.

[4] Moravcsik, 1995; 1998.

[5] Weiler, 1991.

[6] The principle of attributed competences was clearly stated for the first time outside the jurisprudence of the ECJ by the Maastricht Treaty.

[7] The Court had in the early cases defended a strict restrain to expressly delegated powers; see Weiler, 1991: 2433-4. In *Van Gend & Loos* the Court stated that the Community constitutes 'a new legal order of international law for the benefit of which the states have limited their sovereign rights, albeit in limited fields'; or relating to the Coal and Steel Community 'the Treaty rests on a derogation of sovereignty consented by the member states to supranational jurisdiction for an object strictly determined.' The legal principle at the basis of the Treaty is a principle of limited competence. The Community is a legal person of public law and to this effect it has the necessary legal

capacity to exercise its functions but only those. Joined Cases 7/56, 3-7-57, *Dinecke Algera* v. *Common Assembly of the ECSC*, [1957-58] ECR 39. Even so, one could argue whether a strict enumerative approach was ever intended. That is so if one considers that the original design combined general unlimited objectives (but limited means and instruments) together with institutional balance. Indeed, the Community was empowered (on the basis of the principle of express attribution of powers) with narrower powers in the form of means and instruments (those powers framed in diverse governance regimes for a handful of policy sectors) while at the same time the Community was made 'responsible' for broader general objectives defined mostly in horizontal terms rather than vertically. The relationship with national powers in the general and sectoral Community objectives was not specified but left to be agreed at a later stage and within the framework of the European institutions. Also clauses to allow development of the system itself were inserted (ex Article 235 EEC, now Article 308 EC).

[8] The European Court of Justice also established the doctrine of exclusivity and pre-emption.

[9] Sandholtz, 1993; Bulmer, 1998.

[10] That is, for instance the Commission power to trigger new policy dossiers such as regional policy in the early 1970s independently of IGCs, see Vergés Bausili, 2000.

[11] Hooghe, 1996. Hooghe argues that the Commission transformed EU regional policy from an original 'pork-barrel' intervention based on budgetary transfers, into a European regional policy (where support was conditional on assessment of projects and modulated according to common guidelines, and generally speaking where Community rather than national criteria determined eligibility and allocation of funds).

[12] Stein, 1981; Mancini, 1998.

[13] Webb, 1983.

[14] Mazey and Richardson, 1993.

[15] Jeffery, 1995.

[16] Peters, 1994; Marks *et al*, 1996.

[17] Notably, that the objectives of the proposed action cannot be sufficiently achieved by member states' action in the framework of their constitutional system; and that by reason of the scale or effects of the proposed action, it can therefore be better achieved by action on the part of the Community. Complementary powers are those where both national authorities and Community institutions hold competence, and where Community action is not supreme.

[18] Definition as given by the Convention Working Group on complementary competences: see p. 2 of Convention, Mandate of the Working Group on complementary competences, 31 May 2002, CONV 75/2.

[19] States can also challenge Community abuse of powers before the European Court of Justice (Article 230). This mainly entails a judicial analysis as to whether there is legal base for the Community to act, and/or the legal base used (where there is a choice) by the Commission.

[20] See Directive on animals in zoos.

[21] de Búrca, 2001.

[22] On the other hand, one could ask whether unanimity is a sufficient mechanism to check creeping.

[23] See point 9 of the Protocol.

[24] See Inter-Institutional agreement on the quality of Community legislation.

[25] The notion of administrative and financial impact assessments of regulation is dealt with in the Commission White Paper on Governance [COM(2001) 428 of 25 July 2001] and detailed in the Communication on Better Law-making and Impact Assessments [COM(2002) 275 and 276 of June 2002] and following implementing measures, together with the pledge to 'upgrade' subsidiarity commitments by undertaking wider and more transparent pre-legislative consultations of interested parties.

[26] Well before Maastricht into the early 1990s the Delors II Commission started an action of sensibilisation (Ross, 1995) and changing culture of the Commission.

[27] In 1995 the Commission presented 71 proposals for directives and 290 proposals for regulations. In 2000, the number of Commission's proposals for directives fell to 48, and proposals for regulations to193. See Grevi, 2001.

[28] Grevi, 2001:13.

[29] Directive of 1999 on animals in zoos: Commission had proposed a Recommendation but it became, through the legislative procedure, a Directive.

[30] The provisions on subsidiarity in the EU Treaty can be broadly categorised into those relating to subsidiarity as a principle and its definition (preamble and Article 5); and secondly, on provisions relating to its actual materialisation i.e. its implementation (Protocol No 30 on the application of the principles of subsidiarity and proportionality annexed to the EC Treaty – as modified by the Amsterdam Treaty). Article 5 defines subsidiarity (in paragraph 2) in the context of two other principles: the principle of attribution of powers (paragraph 1) and the principle of proportionality (paragraph 3).

[31] CONV 152/02.

[32] A study by the German Federal Finance Ministry reported on the application of the principle of subsidiarity for 1999 and 2000 that the number of proposal contestable on subsidiarity grounds is very reduced (2 out of 60 new proposals for 1999 and 5 out of 84 for 2000) and that in all these cases the 'contestations' apply to partial aspects of the proposals. See Convention, Groupe de Travail I 'Subsidiarité, Objet: Intervéntion de M. Michele Petite, Directeur Général du Service Juridique de la Commission, à la réunion du groupe, le 17 Juin 2002, Bruxelles, 27 Juin 2002, WGI WD3 p. 6.

[33] The European Court of Justice has annulled acts for violation of the principle of conferment of competence or the principle of proportionality, and for the Commission's choice of legal base, but never on the basis of a violation of the principle of subsidiarity. See evidence given by Advocate General Jacobs to WG on subsidiarity: Secretariat Convention: Note. Working Group I on the Principle of Subsidiarity, Summary of the meeting of 25 June 2002, Brussels 28 June 2002, CONV 156/02 WGI 5.

[34] See speech by UK Foreign Affairs Minister Jack Straw in Edinburgh, 27 August 2002.

[35] Case of Directive 93/7/EEC on the return of cultural objects unlawfully removed from the territory of a member state. This is an internal market measure, yet it affects member states' cultural policy (where the Community does not have legislative competence). In the case where a harmonisation measure has been adopted, the member states may retain national provisions justified by certain requirements.

[36] Grevi, 2001.

[37] Convention Praesidium, Draft Protocol on the application of the principles of subsidiarity and proportionality, 27 February 2003, CONV 579/03; and Draft Constitution, Vol I - Revised draft, 26 May 2003, CONV 724/03.

[38] The scrutiny system in the Commons is in a broad sense an early warning system. See

House of Commons, 30th Report, 2001-2002, HC 152-xxx. A separate and different scrutiny system is used in the House of Lords. Peers' scrutiny is a more selective and in depth review of fewer documents. In the UK the different systems are considered complementary.

[39] Other legal appraisals run by the Commons relate to drafting difficulties or the impact of proposals on existing law. These appraisals are likely continue to take place under the early warning system procedures.

[40] The standing order of the European Scrutiny Committee does not require the Committee to assess the merits of EU documents – only their legal or political importance and whether they should be debated. In practice, however, the Committee recognises that 'we do often look at the merits, especially when requesting further information, and the conclusions of our reports sometimes express a general view on a EU proposal. [...] However, we do not usually express views in our Reports on controversial aspects of the merits of documents'. Paragraph §33 House of Commons, 30th Report, 2001-2002, HC 152-xxx.

[41] See paragraph §34 of 30th Report, 2001-2002, HC 152-xxx.

[42] See Maurer,1999.

[43] See paragraph §8 of the Draft Protocol on the application of the principles of subsidiarity and proportionality, 27 February 2003, CONV 579/03.

[44] In the UK a scrutiny reserve resolution can be passed by the House. It constrains ministers from agreeing in Council to legislative proposals and certain other proposals if the Committee has not cleared them or (when the Committee has recommended a document for debate) if the House has not yet come to a resolution concerning them. Exceptions are provided for in the resolution, including 'special reasons', but in such cases the minister must explain the reasons at the earliest opportunity (or to the House if a proposal is awaiting consideration by the House).

[45] Contributions defending subsidiarity being controlled *ex post* by a judicial body: Convention, Contribution by E. Brok, J. Santer, R. van der Linden and J. Wuermeling and other members: 'Subsidiarity must be controlled by a judicial body', Brussels, 24 July 2002, CONV 213/02 CONTRIB 72.

[46] Some Convention members have argued against national parliaments being able to take cases on subsidiarity to the Court on the grounds that it would break the unity of the State before the Court, and thus open the door for regional authorities to take cases against the State. However, Article 230 provides for respect for legal procedures and institutional balance.

[47] Weatherill, 1992.

[48] Secretariat, Contribution by Neil MacCormick, alternate member of the Convention 'Subsidiarity, common sense and local knowledge', Brussels, 18 September 2002, CONV 275/02 CONTRIB 94.

An early afterword
Andrew Duff MEP

Valéry Giscard d'Estaing tells the Convention that we should aspire to drafting a constitution that will last the European Union for fifty years. We listen intently. One of the more remarkable phenomena of the entirely remarkable Convention on the Future of Europe is the transformation of French European policy. France's former President truly reflects this. The death of classical Gaullism, after all, is something of a Giscardien victory.

Peter Hain, on the other hand, the UK government representative in the Convention, has told MPs that the new constitution is 'likely to be a tidying-up exercise [...]. [W]e see it as a consolidation, with some modifications and some changes, of where we have been for many decades.'[1] Silent on the matter of the constitution's durability, the British, who fought to oppose the setting up of the Convention in the first place, are playing their traditional game of seeking to limit the scope of the Convention's work and to dilute the force of its conclusions.

Can the Convention possibly reconcile both views? Only if it sticks to its essential function of the constituent process and avoids wide excursions into the thorny thickets of the detailed reform of EU policies, common or otherwise. The role of a constitution is to establish the institutions and set the legal framework within which they are to make the policy choices. Although the constitution of the Union should lay down its parameters, principles and objectives, it should neither pre-empt nor preclude future political change.

The constitution needs to capture the consensus, certainly, about what the Union is and does. It must be a durable but not an inflexible settlement of where power lies and who exercises it. If the new constitution is to last, it has to allow the Union to evolve as well as entrench. To satisfy public opinion, it will have to articulate not only the anxieties but also the aspirations of the European citizen.

In achieving this clever articulation, the Convention is proving valid and capable. Its composition is broadly representative of the political spectrum. Its working methods have successfully combined both the parliamentary style and the classical diplomatic negotiation. Under the skilful presidency of Giscard, Amato and Dehaene, the Convention has asserted itself. Problematic issues are exposed be they ever so tricky. Bad proposals tend to be eliminated. Compromises are proving possible. It is likely that the consensus that emerges around most of the Convention's proposals will be a fresh one and large. Minority reports will get a poor reception.

Despite the participation of a growing number of national cabinet ministers, the Convention is not captured by member state governments. Despite the vitality and apparent coherence of Members of the European Parliament, they do not drive the Convention's agenda. The preponderance of national parliamentarians has not much blunted the majority federal tendency: the Union will emerge from the Convention with an enhanced competence to act effectively at home and abroad. The large number of *conventionnels* representing the thirteen candidate countries has not deflected the Convention from concentrating on what really matters now to the Union of the Fifteen. The thorough commitment to openness has impressed the media and imposed a certain discipline on most members of the Convention not to say one thing in Brussels and another back home. No member of the Convention will emerge with a set of views identical to that with which they started their work in February 2002. The whole Convention, not excluding its President, has deepened its knowledge of the state of the Union and refined, one hopes accordingly, its prescriptions for change.

Even before its conclusion, therefore, and to complement the work of the first Convention that wrote the Charter of Fundamental Rights in 1999-2000, the Convention has proven to be an institutional success. A return to the old method of the intergovernmental conference (IGC) is frankly inconceivable. No matter that a new IGC will have to complete the constitutive process, the Convention has earned autonomy. The Convention has itself helped to create a new constitutional sovereignty for the Union.

At the time of writing, of course, the Convention is far from home and dry. The consensus on some key issues – the Charter, CFSP, division of competences, the jurisdiction of the Court, the presidency of the Council, the powers of the Parliament, voting procedures in the Council – may yet exclude the government of the United Kingdom.

Much depends on the quality of the second draft of the whole of Part One, expected towards the end of May. In general, the drafting has not been of the highest literary quality. And the Praesidium has shown a lamentable lack of self-confidence in following through in practice the logic of the Convention's decision in principle to merge the three pillars. There is much infelicitous duplication, especially concerning the residuary powers and traditions of the member states, as if their very repetition made those powers and traditions somehow more entrenched. (Instead, it induces a certain unease in the reader.)

The Praesidium is somewhat coy about giving expression to the Convention's general will that qualified majority voting in the Council plus co-decision with the Parliament should be the norm in all law making. It should not be a surprise that some political issues are more sensitive than others. But why there should be many, if any, exceptions to the most democratic and efficient way of doing things is far from clear. There is no equation that says that the Union must apply democracy in inverse proportion to controversy. Clinging to unanimity in the Council because European integration is less mature in one area than in another will not guarantee perfection. On the contrary, in a Union of twenty-five and more member states it threatens sclerosis. It is to be hoped that the Convention will eventually agree to a much wider use of enhanced QMV procedures, with higher thresholds, to replace unanimity even in those areas where eurosceptic governments harbour the greatest reservations.

Difficulties still have to be resolved about how to separate out more clearly the legislative from the executive functions of the Union. A greater separation is a constitutional necessity if simplification is to be assured. Blurring the distinction between the two assists neither comprehension nor legal certainty.

There remains, too, the problem of executive authority of the Union – that most absorbing of constitutional questions of who's in charge.[2] And the aftermath of the invasion of Iraq lies heavy over our final meetings. The Convention might not succeed in providing Europe with a new, post-national constitutional order fit to meet the challenges of the 21st century. But if we fail, it will not only be Europe that is the loser.

Notes

1 Peter Hain speaking to the Foreign Affairs Committee of the House of Commons, 1 April 2003.

2 See the author's article *One Europe, One President* on his website www.andrewduffmep.org, first published in FT.com on 7 April 2003.

Bibliography

Aron, Raymond (1968), *Democracy and Totalitarianism*, London, Weidenfeld & Nicholson.

Barnier, Michel (2002), 'Choisir une Europe sous influence américaine ou une Europe indépendante', *Le Monde* Interview, 23 May.

Bellamy, Richard and Castiglione, Dario (2002), 'Legitimizing the Euro-'Polity' and its 'Regime': The Normative Turn in EU Studies', *European Journal of Political Theory*, 2/1: 7-34.

Bohman, James (1996), *Public Deliberation*, Cambridge, MA, MIT Press.

Bond, Martyn (2002) 'Kerrfully does it', in *The Parliament Magazine*, issue 148, 28 October.

Braibant, Guy (2001), *La charte des droits fondamentaux de l'Union européenne*, Paris, Le Seuil.

Brand, Michiel (2003), 'Towards the Definitive Status of the Charter of Fundamental Rights of the European Union: Political Document or Legally Binding Text?', *German Law Journal* 4/4: 395-409.

de Búrca, Gráinne (1999), 'The Institutional Development of the EU: A Constitutional Analysis', in P. Craig and G. de Búrca, *The Evolution of EU Law*, Oxford, Oxford University Press.

de Búrca, Gráinne (2001), 'Setting Constitutional limits to EU competence', Working paper 1001/02, Faculdade de Direito da Universidade Nova de Lisboa, Francisco Pires Working Papers on European Constitutionalism.

de Búrca, Gráinne (2003), 'Fundamental Rights and Citizenship', in de Witte (2003).

de Búrca, Gráinne and de Witte, Bruno (2001), 'The Delimitation of Powers between the EU and its Member States', Robert Shuman Centre Policy Papers Series on Constitutional Reform of the European Union, WP 2001/03.

Christiansen, Thomas and Jørgensen, Knud Enk (1998), 'Negotiating Treaty Reform in the European Union: The Role of the European Commission', in *International Negotiations*: 435-452.

Church, Clive and Phinnemore, David (2002), *The Penguin Guide to the European Treaties*, London, Penguin Books.

Closa, Carlos (2003), 'Improving EU Constitutional Politics? A Preliminary Assessment of the Convention', *Constitutionalism Web-Papers*, ConWEB, 2003/1, http://les1.man.ac.uk/conweb.

Craig, Paul (1999), 'The Nature of the Community: Integration, Democracy and Legitimacy', in Paul Craig and Grainne de Búrca (eds.), *The Evolution of EU Law*, Oxford, Oxford University Press.

Crum, Ben (2003), 'Towards Finality? A preliminary assessment of the achievements of the European Convention', *ARENA Working Paper*, 03/4, www.arena.ui.no.

Declaration on the Future of the Union, No.: 3 and 4, Official Journal of the European Community, C 80/85, 10 March 2001.The Laeken Declaration, http://European-convention.eu.int/pdf/LKNEN.pdf.

Dehaene, Jean-Luc (2003), 'Towards a Constitutional Treaty for the European Union', Speech to Kings College London, Centre for European Law, 11 February.

Deloche-Gaudez, Florence (2002), 'La Convention pour l'élaboration de la charte des droits fondamentaux : une méthode constituante ?', in Renaud Dehousse (ed.), *Une constitution pour l'Europe ?*, Paris, Presses de sciences-po.

Der Kurier (2002), 'Voggenhuber probt den Aufstand im Konvent,' 21 May 2002.

Die Presse (2002), 'Frankreich und Grossbritannien wollen EU-Präsidenten installieren,' 17 May 2002.

Dougan, Michael (2003), 'Some Comments on the Praesidium's 'Draft Treaty Establishing a Constitution for Europe", Federal Trust Online Constitutionalism Essay, No. 7, March 2003, www.fedtrust.co.uk/eu_constitution.

Dryzek, John (2000), *Deliberative Democracy and Beyond, Liberals, Critics, Contestations*, Oxford, Oxford University Press.

Duff, Andrew (2003), 'The Convention: approaching the endgame', Interview with Giovanni Grevi, *Challenge Europe*, www.theepc.be, 6 March.

Duff, Andrew (2003), 'One Europe, One President', *Financial Times*, 7 April.

Elster, Jon (1994), 'Argumenter et négocier dans deux assemblées constituantes', *Revue française de science politique*, 44/2: 187-256.

Elster, Jon (ed.) (1998a), *Deliberative Democracy*, Cambridge, Cambridge University Press.

Elster, Jon (1998b), 'Deliberation and Constitution-Making', in Jon Elster (ed.), *Deliberative Democracy*, Oxford, Oxford University Press.

EU Observer (2001), 'How the 15 agreed on Giscard d'Estaing,' 17 December.

EU Observer (2002), 'Giscard likes reform fever in EU institutions,' 22 June, http://www.euobserver.com/index.phtml?sid=9&aid=6752.

European Parliament, Lamassoure Report, *A-0133/2002*.

Feus, Kim (ed.) (2001), *A Simplified Treaty for the European Union?*, London, The Federal Trust.

Fischer, Joschka (2000), 'From Confederation to Federation – Thoughts on the Finality of European Integration', Speech given at the Humboldt University zu Berlin, Germany, 12 May, The Federal Trust *European Essay* No.8.

Fishkin, James (1995), *The Voice of the People*, New Haven, Yale University Press.

Gerstenberg, Oliver and Sabel, Charles (2002), 'Directly Deliberative Polyarchy: An Institutional Ideal for Europe?', in Christian Joerges and Renaud Dehousse (eds.), *Good Governance in Europe's Integrated Market*, Oxford, Oxford University Press.

Giscard d'Estaing, Valéry and Schmidt, Helmut (2000), 'Time to Slow Down and Consolidate Around 'Euro-Europe'', *International Herald Tribune*, 11 April.

Giscard d'Estaing, Valéry (2002a), 'Introductory Speech to the Convention on the Future of Europe', SN 1565/02, Brussels, 26 February (delivered 28 February).

Giscard d'Estaing, Valéry, (2002b), http://European-convention.eu.int.

Giscard d'Estaing, Valéry (2002c) 'La derniere chance de l'Europe unie,' *Le Monde*, 23. July 2002.

Giscard d'Estaing, Valéry (2002d) 'Interview with Valéry Giscard d'Estaing,' *Financial Times*, 07. October 2002.

Grevi, Giovanni (2001), 'Beyond the delimitation of competences: implementing subsidiarity', *The Europe We Need – Working Paper*, European Policy Centre, 25 September 2001.

Pleuger, Gunter (2001), 'Der Vertrag von Nizza: Gesamtbewertung der Ergebnisse', in Mathias Jopp, Barbara Lippert and Heinrich Schneider (eds.) (2001), *Das Vertragswerk von Nizza und die Zukunft der Europäischen Union*, Berlin.

Habermas, Jürgen (1996), *Between Facts and Norms, Contributions to a Discourse Theory of Law and Democracy*, Cambridge, MA, MIT Press.

Habermas, Jürgen (2001), 'Why Europe needs a Constitution?', *New Left Review*, 11: 5-26.

Hain, Peter (2003), 'The Future of Europe: A Union of Sovereign States', Speech, Adjournment Debate, Westminster Hall, London, 20 March.

Hooghe, Liesbet (ed.) (1996), *Cohesion Policy, the European Community and Subnational Government*, Oxford, Oxford University Press.

House of Commons (2002), 'European Scrutiny in the Commons', 30th Report of the Session 2001-2002, 22 May 2002, HC 152- xxx.

Convention on the Future of Europe – First Progress Report from the UK National Parliament Representatives, 30 April 2002(a)

Convention on the Future of Europe – Second Progress Report from the UK National Parliament Representatives, 20 June 2002(b)

Howse, Robert and Nicolaïdis, Kalypso (eds.) (2000), *The Federal Vision*, Oxford, Oxford University Press.

Hughes, Kirsty (2003), 'The Institutional Debate: Who is Pre-empting the Convention?', *EPIN Convention Comment*, http://www.epin.org/convention/comment.html.

Jeffery, Charlie (1995), 'Regional Information Offices and the Politics of the 'Third Level' Lobbying in Brussels', Paper presented to UACES Conference.

Kohler-Koch, Beate (1999), 'A Constitution for Europe?', Working Paper of the Mannheim Centre for European Social Research, 8/1999.

Lefort, Claude (1988), *Democracy and Political Theory*, Cambridge/Oxford, Polity/Blackwell.

Lijphart, Arend (1999), *Patterns of Democracy*, New Haven, Yale University Press.

Lodge, Juliet (1998), 'Intergovernmental Conferences and European Integration: Negotiating the Amsterdam Treaty', in *International Negotiations*, No 3: 345-362.

Lord, Chris and Magnette, Paul (2001), 'E Pluribus Unum ? Notes towards a General Theory of Legitimacy in the EU', *ESRC One Europe or Several Working Papers*, 39/02.

Magnette Paul (2002), *Deliberation vs. negotiation*, Paper prepared for the First Pan-European Conference of the ECPR Standing Group on the European Union, Bordeaux 26-28 September.

Magnette, Paul (2003), 'European Governance and Civic Participation: Beyond Elitist Citizenship?', *Political Studies*, 52/1: 1-17.

Majone, Giandomenico (1996) (ed.), *Regulating Europe*, London/New York, Routledge.

Majone, Giandomenico (2001), 'Nonmajoritarian Institutions and the Limits of Democratic Governance: A Political Transaction-Cost Approach', *Journal of Institutional and Theoretical Economics*, 157/1: 57-78.

Mancini, G. Federico (1989), 'The making of a constitution for Europe', *Common Market Law Review*, 26: 595-614.

Manin, Bernard (1998), *Principles of Representative Government*, Cambridge, Cambridge University Press.

Marks, Gary, Nielsen, François, Ray, Leonard and Salk, Jane (1996), 'Competencies, cracks and conflicts: regional mobilization in the European Union', in G. Marks, F.W. Scharpf, P.C. Schmitter and W. Streeck (1996) *Governance in the European Union*, London, Sage: 40-63.

Maurer, Andreas (1999), *What next for the European Parliament?*, London, Federal Trust Series: Future of European Parliamentary Democracy 2.

Mazey, Sonia and Richardson, Jeremy (1993), *Lobbying in the European Community*, Oxford, Oxford University Press.

Monar, Jörg and Wessels Wolfgang (eds) (2001), *The European Union after the Treaty of Amsterdam*, London, Continuum.

Moravcsik, Andrew (2002), 'In Defence of 'Democratic deficit': Reassessing Legitimacy in the European Union', *Journal of Common Market Studies*, 40/4: 603-24.

Moravcsik, Andrew (1998), *The Choice for Europe*, Ithaca, Cornell University Press.

Moravcsik, Andrew and Nicolaïdis, Kalypso (1998), 'Keynote Article: Federal Ideals and Constitutional Realities in the Treaty of Amsterdam', *Journal of Common Market Studies: Annual Review*, 36: 13-38.

Ophuls, Carl Friedrich (1966), 'Zur ideengeschichtlichen Herkunft der Gemeinschaftsverfassung', in E. von Caemmerer, H.-J. Schlochauer and E. Steindorff (eds.), *Probleme des Europäischen Rechts*, Festschrift für Walter Hallstein zu seinem 65. Geburtstag, Frankfurt-am-Main, Vittorio Klostermann.

Perelman, Chaïm and Olbrechts-Tyteca, Lucie (1969), *The New Rhetoric, A Treatise on Argumentation*, Notre Dame, University of Notre Dame Press.

Pernice, Ingolf (2002), *De la constitution composée de l'Europe*, RTEurope 36: 623-647

Peters, B. Guy (1994), 'Agenda-setting in the European Community', *Journal of European Public Policy*, 1/1: 9-26.

Przeworski, Adam, Stokes, Susan C. and Manin, Bernard (1999) (eds.), *Democracy, Accountability and Representation*, Cambridge, Cambridge University Press.

Rawls, John (1993), *Political Liberalism*, New York, Columbia University Press.

Robert Schuman Centre for Advanced Studies (European University Institute, Florence) (2000), *A Basic Treaty for the European Union. A Study of the Reorganization of the Treaties* (study co-ordinated by Y. Mény and C.-D. Ehlermann), May 2000 (http://europa.eu.int/comm/archives/igc2000/offdoc/discussiondocs).

Sandholtz, Wayne (1993), 'Choosing union: monetary politics and Maastricht', *International Organization*, 47/1.

Sartori, Giovanni (1965), *Democratic Theory*, New York, Praeger.

Scharpf, Fritz (1998), *Governing in Europe, Effective and Democratic*, Oxford, Oxford University Press.

Shaw, Jo (2000a), *Law of the European Union*, London, Palgrave, 3rd Edition.

Shaw, Jo (2000b), 'Relating Constitutionalism and flexibility in the EU', in Gráinne de Búrca and Joanne Scott (eds.), *Constitutional Change in the EU: From Uniformity to Flexibility?*, Oxford, Hart Publishing: 337-358.

Shaw, Jo (2002), 'Notes on the Praesidium's Preliminary Draft Constitution', *Federal Trust Constitutionalism Online Essay*, No. 9 (www.fedtrust.co.uk/eu_constitution).

Shaw, Jo (2003), 'Process, Responsibility and Inclusion in EU Constitutionalism', *European Law Journal* 9/1: 45-68.

Stein, Eric (1981), 'Lawyers, judges and the making of a transnational constitution', *American Journal of International Law*, 75/ 1: 1-27.

Straw, Jack (2001), 'Europe after 11 September', At the Royal Institute of International Affairs, 11 December, http://www.fco.gov.uk/servlet/Front?pagename=OpenMarket/Xcelerate/ShowPage&c=Page&cid=1007029391647&a =KArticle&aid=1013618415734.

Sunstein, Cass (2001), *Designing Democracy, What Constitutions Do*, Oxford, Oxford University Press.

Tizzano, Antonio (1983), 'The powers of the Community', in VVAA *Thirty years of Community law*, The European Perspectives Series, Luxembourg: Office for Official Publications.

de Tocqueville, Alexis (1889), *Democracy in America*, London and New York, Longmans and Green.

Vergés Bausili, Anna (2000), 'The emergence, construction and negotiation of a regional competence for the Community', PhD thesis, University of Edinburgh.

Von Bogdandy, Armin (2000), 'The European Union as a Supranational Federation: A Conceptual Attempt in the Light of the Amsterdam Treaty', *Columbia Journal of European Law*, 6/1: 27-54.

Weatherill, Stephen (1992a), *Cases and materials on EC Law*, London, Blackstone Press.

Weatherill, Stephen (2003a), 'Using National Parliaments to improve Scrutiny of EC/EU action', *Jurist EU 'Thinking Outside the Box' Editorial Series*, Paper 02/2003 (http://www.fd.unl.pt/je/edit_pap2003-02.htm).

Weatherill, Stephen (2003b), 'Competences', in Bruno de Witte (ed.), *Ten Reflections on the Constitutional Treaty for Europe*, Robert Schuman Centre for Advanced Studies (European University Institute): San Domenico di Fiesole.

Webb, Carole (1983), 'Theoretical perspectives and problems', in H. Wallace, W. Wallace and C. Webb (eds.), *Policy making in the European Communities*, London, John Wiley.

Weiler, Joseph H. H. (1991), 'The Transformation of Europe', *Yale Law Journal*, 100: 2403-2483.

Weiler, Joseph H. H. (2001), 'Federalism with Constitutionalism: Europe's *Sonderweg*', in Kalyspo Nicolaïdes and Robert Howse (eds.), *The Federal Vision. Legitimacy and Levels of Governance in the United States and the European Union*, Oxford, Oxford University Press: 54-70.

Weiler, Joseph H. H. (2002), 'A Constitution for Europe? Some Hard Choices', *Journal of Common Market Studies*, 40/4: 563-580.

Weiler, Joseph H. H. (1999), *The Constitution of Europe*, Cambridge, Cambridge University Press.

Wessels, Wolfgang (2001) 'Nice Results: The Millennium IGC in the EU's Evolution', in *Journal of Common Market Studies*, 39/ -2: 197-219.

de Witte, Bruno (2002), 'The Closest Thing to a Constitutional Conversation in Europe: the Semi-Permanent Treaty Revision Process', in Paul Beaumont, Carole Lyons and Neil Walker (eds.), *Convergence and Divergence in European Public Law*, Oxford, Hart Publishing: 39-57.

de Witte, Bruno (ed.) (2003), *Ten Reflections on the Constitutional Treaty for Europe*, Robert Schuman Centre for Advanced Studies (European University Institute): San Domenico di Fiesole, e-book, www.iue.it/rscac.

Yataganas, Xénophon A. (2001) 'The Treaty of Nice – The Sharing of Power and the Institutional Balance in the European Union – A Constitutional Perspective', in *European Law Journal*, 7/3: 242-291.

Appendices

Declaration on the Future of the Union
Declaration 23, Treaty of Nice, 26 February 2001, OJ C 80/85

1. Important reforms have been decided in Nice. The Conference welcomes the successful conclusion of the Conference of Representatives of the Governments of the Member States and commits the Member States to pursue the early and successful ratification of the Treaty of Nice.

2. It agrees that the conclusion of the Conference of Representatives of the Governments of the Member States opens the way for enlargement of the European Union and underlines that, with ratification of the Nice Treaty, the European Union will have completed the institutional changes necessary for the accession of new Member States.

3. Having opened the way to enlargement, the Conference calls for a deeper and wider debate about the future development of the European Union. In 2001, the Swedish and Belgian Presidencies, in co-operation with the Commission and involving the European Parliament, will encourage wide-ranging discussions with all interested parties; representatives of national Parliaments and all those reflecting public opinion; political, economic and university circles, representatives of civil society, etc. The candidate States will be associated with this process in ways to be defined.

4. Following a report to Göteborg in June 2001, the European Council, at its meeting at Laeken/Brussels in December 2001, will agree on a declaration containing appropriate initiatives for the continuation of this process.

5. The process should address, inter alia, the following questions:

• how to establish and monitor a more precise delimitation of competencies between the European Union and the Member States, reflecting the principle of subsidiarity;

• the status of the Charter of Fundamental Rights of the European Union proclaimed in Nice, in accordance with the conclusions of the European Council in Cologne;

• a simplification of the Treaties with a view to making them clearer and better understood without changing their meaning;

• the role of national Parliaments in the European architecture.

6. Addressing the above-mentioned issues, the Conference recognises the need to improve and to monitor the democratic legitimacy and transparency of the Union and its institutions, to bring them closer to the citizens of the Member States.

7. After these preparatory steps, the Conference agrees that a new Conference of the Representatives of the Governments of the Member States will be convened in 2004, to treat the above-mentioned items in view of the related Treaty changes.

8. The Conference of Member States shall not constitute any form of obstacle or pre-condition to the enlargement process. Moreover, those candidate States which have concluded accession negotiations with the Union shall be invited to participate in the Conference. Those candidate States which have not concluded their accession negotiations shall be invited as observers.

The Future of the European Union
Laeken Declaration
15 December 2001

I. Europe at a Crossroads

For centuries, peoples and states have taken up arms and waged war to win control of the European continent. The debilitating effects of two bloody wars and the weakening of Europe's position in the world brought a growing realisation that only peace and concerted action could make the dream of a strong, unified Europe come true. In order to banish once and for all the demons of the past, a start was made with a coal and steel community. Other economic activities, such as agriculture, were subsequently added in. A genuine single market was eventually established for goods, persons, services and capital, and a single currency was added in 1999. On 1 January 2002 the euro is to become a day-to-day reality for 300 million European citizens.

The European Union has thus gradually come into being. In the beginning, it was more of an economic and technical collaboration. Twenty years ago, with the first direct elections to the European Parliament, the Community's democratic legitimacy, which until then had lain with the Council alone, was considerably strengthened. Over the last ten years, construction of a political union has begun and co-operation been established on social policy, employment, asylum, immigration, police, justice, foreign policy and a common security and defence policy.

The European Union is a success story. For over half a century now, Europe has been at peace. Along with North America and Japan, the Union forms one of the three most prosperous parts of the world. As a result of mutual solidarity and fair distribution of the benefits of economic development, moreover, the standard of living in the Union's weaker regions has increased enormously and they have made good much of the disadvantage they were at.

Fifty years on, however, the Union stands at a crossroads, a defining moment in its existence. The unification of Europe is near. The Union is about to expand to bring in more than ten new Member States, predominantly Central and Eastern European, thereby finally closing one of the darkest chapters in European history: the Second World War and the ensuing artificial division of Europe. At long last, Europe is on its way to becoming one big family, without bloodshed, a real transformation clearly calling for a different approach from fifty years ago, when six countries first took the lead.

The democratic challenge facing Europe

At the same time, the Union faces twin challenges, one within and the other beyond its borders.

Within the Union, the European institutions must be brought closer to its citizens. Citizens undoubtedly support the Union's broad aims, but they do not always see a connection between those goals and the Union's everyday action. They want the

European institutions to be less unwieldy and rigid and, above all, more efficient and open. Many also feel that the Union should involve itself more with their particular concerns, instead of intervening, in every detail, in matters by their nature better left to Member States' and regions' elected representatives. This is even perceived by some as a threat to their identity. More importantly, however, they feel that deals are all too often cut out of their sight and they want better democratic scrutiny.

Europe's new role in a globalised world

Beyond its borders, in turn, the European Union is confronted with a fast-changing, globalised world. Following the fall of the Berlin Wall, it looked briefly as though we would for a long while be living in a stable world order, free from conflict, founded upon human rights. Just a few years later, however, there is no such certainty. The eleventh of September has brought a rude awakening. The opposing forces have not gone away: religious fanaticism, ethnic nationalism, racism and terrorism are on the increase, and regional conflicts, poverty and underdevelopment still provide a constant seedbed for them.

What is Europe's role in this changed world? Does Europe not, now that is finally unified, have a leading role to play in a new world order, that of a power able both to play a stabilising role world-wide and to point the way ahead for many countries and peoples? Europe as the continent of humane values, the Magna Carta, the Bill of Rights, the French Revolution and the fall of the Berlin Wall; the continent of liberty, solidarity and above all diversity, meaning respect for others' languages, cultures and traditions. The European Union's one boundary is democracy and human rights. The Union is open only to countries which uphold basic values such as free elections, respect for minorities and respect for the rule of law.

Now that the Cold War is over and we are living in a globalised, yet also highly fragmented world, Europe needs to shoulder its responsibilities in the governance of globalisation. The role it has to play is that of a power resolutely doing battle against all violence, all terror and all fanaticism, but which also does not turn a blind eye to the world's heartrending injustices. In short, a power wanting to change the course of world affairs in such a way as to benefit not just the rich countries but also the poorest. A power seeking to set globalisation within a moral framework, in other words to anchor it in solidarity and sustainable development.

The expectations of Europe's citizens

The image of a democratic and globally engaged Europe admirably matches citizens' wishes. There have been frequent public calls for a greater EU role in justice and security, action against cross-border crime, control of migration flows and reception of asylum seekers and refugees from far-flung war zones. Citizens also want results in the fields of employment and combating poverty and social exclusion, as well as in the field of economic and social cohesion. They want a common approach on environmental pollution, climate change and food safety, in short, all transnational issues which they instinctively sense can only be tackled by working together. Just as they also want to see Europe more involved in foreign affairs, security and defence, in other words, greater and better co-ordinated action to deal with trouble spots in and around Europe and in the rest of the world.

At the same time, citizens also feel that the Union is behaving too bureaucratically in numerous other areas. In co-ordinating the economic, financial and fiscal environment, the basic issue should continue to be proper operation of the internal market and the single currency, without this jeopardising Member States' individuality. National and regional differences frequently stem from history or tradition. They can be enriching. In other words, what citizens understand by 'good governance' is opening up fresh opportunities, not imposing further red tape. What they expect is more results, better responses to practical issues and not a European superstate or European institutions inveigling their way into every nook and cranny of life.

In short, citizens are calling for a clear, open, effective, democratically controlled Community approach, developing a Europe which points the way ahead for the world. An approach that provides concrete results in terms of more jobs, better quality of life, less crime, decent education and better health care. There can be no doubt that this will require Europe to undergo renewal and reform.

II. Challenges and Reforms in a Renewed Union

The Union needs to become more democratic, more transparent and more efficient. It also has to resolve three basic challenges: how to bring citizens, and primarily the young, closer to the European design and the European institutions, how to organise politics and the European political area in an enlarged Union and how to develop the Union into a stabilising factor and a model in the new, multipolar world. In order to address them a number of specific questions need to be put.

A better division and definition of competence in the European Union

Citizens often hold expectations of the European Union that are not always fulfilled. And vice versa - they sometimes have the impression that the Union takes on too much in areas where its involvement is not always essential. Thus the important thing is to clarify, simplify and adjust the division of competence between the Union and the Member States in the light of the new challenges facing the Union. This can lead both to restoring tasks to the Member States and to assigning new missions to the Union, or to the extension of existing powers, while constantly bearing in mind the equality of the Member States and their mutual solidarity.

A first series of questions that needs to be put concerns how the division of competence can be made more transparent. Can we thus make a clearer distinction between three types of competence: the exclusive competence of the Union, the competence of the Member States and the shared competence of the Union and the Member States? At what level is competence exercised in the most efficient way? How is the principle of subsidiarity to be applied here? And should we not make it clear that any powers not assigned by the Treaties to the Union fall within the exclusive sphere of competence of the Member States? And what would be the consequences of this?

The next series of questions should aim, within this new framework and while respecting the *acquis communautaire*, to determine whether there needs to be any reorganisation of competence. How can citizens' expectations be taken as a guide here? What missions would this produce for the Union? And, vice versa, what tasks could better be left to the Member States? What amendments should be made to the Treaty on the various policies? How, for example, should a more coherent common foreign policy and defence policy be developed? Should the Petersberg tasks be updated? Do we want to adopt a more integrated approach to police and criminal law co-operation? How can economic-policy co-ordination be stepped up? How can we intensify co-operation in the field of social inclusion, the environment, health and food safety? But then, should not the day-to-day administration and implementation of the Union's policy be left more emphatically to the Member States and, where their constitutions so provide, to the regions? Should they not be provided with guarantees that their spheres of competence will not be affected?

Lastly, there is the question of how to ensure that a redefined division of competence does not lead to a creeping expansion of the competence of the Union or to encroachment upon the exclusive areas of competence of the Member States and, where there is provision for this, regions. How are we to ensure at the same time that the European dynamic does not come to a halt? In the future as well the Union must continue to be able to react to fresh challenges and developments and must be able to explore new policy areas. Should Articles 95 and 308 of the Treaty be reviewed for this purpose in the light of the *acquis jurisprudentiel*?

Simplification of the Union's instruments

Who does what is not the only important question; the nature of the Union's action and what instruments it should use are equally important. Successive amendments to the Treaty have on each occasion resulted in a proliferation of instruments, and directives have gradually evolved towards more and more detailed legislation. The key question is therefore whether the Union's various instruments should not be better defined and whether their number should not be reduced.

In other words, should a distinction be introduced between legislative and executive measures? Should the number of legislative instruments be reduced: directly applicable rules, framework legislation and non-enforceable instruments (opinions, recommendations, open co-ordination)? Is it or is it not desirable to have more frequent recourse to framework legislation, which affords the Member States more room for manoeuvre in achieving policy objectives? For which areas of competence are open co-ordination and mutual recognition the most appropriate instruments? Is the principle of proportionality to remain the point of departure?

More democracy, transparency and efficiency in the European Union

The European Union derives its legitimacy from the democratic values it projects, the aims it pursues and the powers and instruments it possesses. However, the European project also derives its legitimacy from democratic, transparent and efficient institutions. The national parliaments also contribute towards the legitimacy of the European project. The declaration on the future of the Union, annexed to the Treaty of Nice, stressed the need to examine their role in European integration. More generally, the question arises as to what initiatives we can take to develop a European public area.

The first question is thus how we can increase the democratic legitimacy and transparency of the present institutions, a question which is valid for the three institutions.

How can the authority and efficiency of the European Commission be enhanced? How should the President of the Commission be appointed: by the European Council, by the European Parliament or should he be directly elected by the citizens? Should the role of the European Parliament be strengthened? Should we extend the right of co-decision or not? Should the way in which we elect the members of the European Parliament be reviewed? Should a European electoral constituency be created, or should constituencies continue to be determined nationally? Can the two systems be combined? Should the role of the Council be strengthened? Should the Council act in the same manner in its legislative and its executive capacities? With a view to greater transparency, should the meetings of the Council, at least in its legislative capacity, be public? Should citizens have more access to Council documents? How, finally, should the balance and reciprocal control between the institutions be ensured?

A second question, which also relates to democratic legitimacy, involves the role of national parliaments. Should they be represented in a new institution, alongside the Council and the European Parliament? Should they have a role in areas of European action in which the European Parliament has no competence? Should they focus on the division of competence between Union and Member States, for example through preliminary checking of compliance with the principle of subsidiarity?

The third question concerns how we can improve the efficiency of decision-making and the workings of the institutions in a Union of some thirty Member States. How could the Union set its objectives and priorities more effectively and ensure better implementation? Is there a need for more decisions by a qualified majority? How is the co-decision procedure between the Council and the European Parliament to be simplified and speeded up? What of the six-monthly rotation of the Presidency of the Union? What is the future role of the European Parliament? What of the future role and structure of the various Council formations? How should the coherence of European foreign policy be enhanced? How is synergy between the High Representative and the competent Commissioner to be reinforced? Should the external representation of the Union in international fora be extended further?

Towards a Constitution for European citizens

The European Union currently has four Treaties. The objectives, powers and policy instruments of the Union are currently spread across those Treaties. If we are to have greater transparency, simplification is essential.

Four sets of questions arise in this connection. The first concerns simplifying the existing Treaties without changing their content. Should the distinction between the Union and the Communities be reviewed? What of the division into three pillars?

Questions then arise as to the possible reorganisation of the Treaties. Should a distinction be made between a basic treaty and the other treaty provisions? Should this distinction involve separating the texts? Could this lead to a distinction between the amendment and ratification procedures for the basic treaty and for the other treaty provisions?

Thought would also have to be given to whether the Charter of Fundamental Rights should be included in the basic treaty and to whether the European Community should accede to the European Convention on Human Rights.

The question ultimately arises as to whether this simplification and reorganisation might not lead in the long run to the adoption of a constitutional text in the Union. What might the basic features of such a constitution be? The values which the Union cherishes, the fundamental rights and obligations of its citizens, the relationship between Member States in the Union?

III. CONVENING OF A CONVENTION ON THE FUTURE OF EUROPE

In order to pave the way for the next Intergovernmental Conference as broadly and openly as possible, the European Council has decided to convene a Convention composed of the main parties involved in the debate on the future of the Union. In the light of the foregoing, it will be the task of that Convention to consider the key issues arising for the Union's future development and try to identify the various possible responses.

The European Council has appointed Mr V. Giscard d'Estaing as Chairman of the Convention and Mr G. Amato and Mr J.L. Dehaene as Vice-Chairmen.

Composition

In addition to its Chairman and Vice-Chairmen, the Convention will be composed of 15 representatives of the Heads of State or Government of the Member States (one from each Member State), 30 members of national parliaments (two from each Member State), 16 members of the European Parliament and two Commission representatives. The accession candidate countries will be fully involved in the Convention's proceedings. They will be represented in the same way as the current Member States (one government representative and two national parliament members) and will be able to take part in the proceedings without, however, being able to prevent any consensus which may emerge among the Member States.

The members of the Convention may only be replaced by alternate members if they are not present. The alternate members will be designated in the same way as full members.

The Praesidium of the Convention will be composed of the Convention Chairman and Vice-Chairmen and nine members drawn from the Convention (the representatives of all the governments holding the Council Presidency during the Convention, two national parliament representatives, two European Parliament representatives and two Commission representatives).

Three representatives of the Economic and Social Committee with three representatives of the European social partners; from the Committee of the Regions: six representatives (to be appointed by the Committee of the Regions from the regions, cities and regions with legislative powers), and the European Ombudsman will be invited to attend as observers. The Presidents of the Court of Justice and of the Court of Auditors may be invited by the Praesidium to address the Convention.

Length of proceedings

The Convention will hold its inaugural meeting on 1 March 2002, when it will appoint its Praesidium and adopt its rules of procedure. Proceedings will be completed after a year, that is to say in time for the Chairman of the Convention to present its outcome to the European Council.

Working methods

The Chairman will pave the way for the opening of the Convention's proceedings by drawing conclusions from the public debate. The Praesidium will serve to lend impetus and will provide the Convention with an initial working basis.

The Praesidium may consult Commission officials and experts of its choice on any technical aspect which it sees fit to look into. It may set up ad hoc working parties.

The Council will be kept informed of the progress of the Convention's proceedings. The Convention Chairman will give an oral progress report at each European Council meeting, thus enabling Heads of State or Government to give their views at the same time.

The Convention will meet in Brussels. The Convention's discussions and all official documents will be in the public domain. The Convention will work in the Union's eleven working languages.

Final document

The Convention will consider the various issues. It will draw up a final document which may comprise either different options, indicating the degree of support which they received, or recommendations if consensus is achieved.

Together with the outcome of national debates on the future of the Union, the final document will provide a starting point for discussions in the Intergovernmental Conference, which will take the ultimate decisions.

Forum

In order for the debate to be broadly based and involve all citizens, a Forum will be opened for organisations representing civil society (the social partners, the business world, non-governmental organisations, academia, etc.). It will take the form of a structured network of organisations receiving regular information on the Convention's proceedings. Their contributions will serve as input into the debate. Such organisations may be heard or consulted on specific topics in accordance with arrangements to be established by the Praesidium.

Secretariat

The Praesidium will be assisted by a Convention Secretariat, to be provided by the General Secretariat of the Council, which may incorporate Commission and European Parliament experts.